# Walkabout

Frontier Life in the 1930s

Ion Idriess

ETT IMPRINT
Exile Bay

First published by ETT Imprint, Exile Bay in 2024

Copyright © Idriess Enterprises 2024

Compiled by Tom Thompson

This book is copyright. Apart from any fair dealing for the purposes of private study, research, criticism or review, as permitted under the Copyright Act, no part may be reproduced by any process without written permission. Enquiries should be addressed to the publisher, or by email to ettimprint@hotmail.com

ETT IMPRINT
PO Box R1906
Royal Exchange NSW 1225
Australia

ISBN 978-1-923205-55-0 (hard)

ISBN 978-1-923205-33-8 (paper)

ISBN 978-1-923205-34-5 (ebook)

Design by Tom Thompson

for Peter & Hillary Shead

Ion Idriess.

# Contents

Ion Idriess - by Himself  *7*
1 The Kimberleys  *10*
2 Where the Wild Men Roam  *15*
3 Arnhem Land  *23*
4 Darwin, North Australia  *29*
5 West of the Darling  *35*
6 Sand  *41*
7 Lazy Days in Crocodile Land  *49*
8 Pearls  *59*
9 Romance of the Coral Seas  *73*
10 The Amazon Gins  *80*
11 Rats  *84*
12 A Series of Plagues  *87*
13 Billy Crystal  *92*

# WALKABOUT

*The title has an "age-old" background and signifies a racial characteristic of the Australian aboriginal who is always on the move. And so, month by month, through the medium of pen and picture, this journal will take you on a great "walkabout" through a new and fascinating world below the Equator.*

These stories were originally published in *Walkabout Magazine*.

1 The Kimberleys - 1st November 1934, pp 32-34
2 Where the Wild Men Roam - 1st January 1935, pp 17-22
3 Arnhem Land - 1st February 1935, pp 31-33
4 Darwin, North Australia - 1st March 1935, pp 37-39
5 West of the Darling - 1st August 1935, pp 41-43
6 Sand - 1st September 1935, pp 22-24
7 Lazy Days in Crocodile Land - 1st November 1936, pp11-15
8 Pearls - 1st October 1937, pp 13-18
9 Romance of the Coral Seas - 1st December 1938, pp 19-21

10 *Sydney Morning Herald* - 6 January 1936, p8 as Matriarch Gins.
11 Unpublished story 1935
12 *Sydney Morning Herald* - 5 July 1935, page 11
13 *Sydney Morning Herald* - 25 April 1936, page 11
    also *Pacific Islands Monthly*, May 22 1936, page 50

# ION IDRIESS

## *by Himself*

IDRIESS, Ion Llewelyn (N.S.W): son of Walter Owen Idriess, Sheriff's Officer; b. Sept. 20 1890; ed. At various NSW schools, principally Broken Hill Public School, School of Mines, Broken Hill; honors in chemistry, certificate in assaying; is author; was assayer's assistant Broken Hill Pty Mine; adventurer, seaman, station hand, drover, track-finder, wharf lumper; was opal miner; opened up the famous "Deadman's Claim" at Lightening Ridge, N.S.W., which became the rich "Hill." Wandered in Northern Queensland, Northern Australia, the Gulf country and the Inland, the Torres Strait Islands and Papua, prospecting for minerals, seeking sandalwood, in a prelude to a wandering life; after locating gold in the unexplored jungle ranges, inland from the Bloomfield, he crossed the Daintree Divide then turned north and travelled bush through Cape York Peninsular, until stopped by the sea at Australia's northern-most limit, Peek Point; sailed the waters of Great Barrier Reef and the Coral Sea with the "Wandering Missionary" and by pearling lugger; with son of Jardine of Somerset sailed 1200 miles in a 27 ft cutter to examine unknown tract in Cape York Peninsular for Queensland Mines Department; cruised the Great Barrier Reef in search of trochus shell, while examining island and mainland for minerals; with a mate was abandoned for seven months on barren Howich Island, where they existed by spearing fish and crabs until rescued by a Japanese pearler; wandered for a time with two different native tribes in Cape York Peninsular studying the people, collecting material for future books, prospecting and roaming generally; worked for wages only from sheer adversity or the urge to learn something new; helped build the automatic light automatic light on Restoration Rock, and was among the picked crew that successfully carried out the greatest cable repair job undertaken in Australia; served Great War A.I.F. Gallipoli, Sinai and Palestine, sniper and scout. Resumed his wandering life. Publications: Madman's Island 1926, Prospecting for Gold 1931, Lasseter's Last Ride 1931, Flynn of the Inland 1932, The Desert Column 1932, Men of the Jungle 1932, Gold Dust and Ashes 1933, Drums of Mer 1933, The Yellow Joss 1934, Man Tracks 1935, Cattle King 1936, Address c/o Angus & Robertson Ltd, 89 Castlereagh Street, Sydney.

from Ion Idriess Archive, 1936

Karadjeri man with pirmal, Kimberley, Western Australia, 1930.
Photograph by Ralph Piddington.

# 1

# The Kimberleys

*North-West Australia*

WEST Australia's pride and yet her puzzle - the Kimberleys. Land of waterless rivers, yet turbulent floods.

Land of the dry, yet of the wet. Of grasses that tower high over man and beast, yet wither fast and fade away. Soil that will grow almost anything if only it has water, yet the seasonal rainfall is large. Land of the bridgeless road that crosses a hundred creeks, of valleys and gorges barred by mountain bastions, over which screech the black cockatoo and where roams only the black man. Land of big cattle herds, yet a puzzle where to sell the meat. A land whose white population dwindles yearly, yet a land that could be made to support a large white population. Time will solve its local problems.

The Kimberleys is the north-western corner of Western Australia, and is divided into East and West Kimberleys, the extreme north-west being often referred to as North-West Kimberley. This region is bounded on the east by the Northern Territory border, on the south by the desert country. Parallel with the desert fringe are the channels of the Margaret, Mary, Louisa, and other watercourses joining up with the Old Man River of the West Kimberleys, the Fitzroy. This reviver of the lowlands runs parallel with the desert fringe right to King Sound at Derby. Along the valleyed banks of this river is the main road of the Kimberleys, with the main stations. In the wet season the Fitzroy is a rolling brown stream, often flooding the country for miles to either side. The river sweeps on for 200 miles, making road and tracks impassable to wheeled transport. In the dry season, its bed holds only an occasional deep water-hole, tree-lined and placid.

The main West Kimberley stations are along the Fitzroy. On the "river" side is Noonkanbah, largest sheep station in Western Australia. On the desert side is Gogo, largest cattle station, which, even under the cattle slump and other difficulties, is successful.

Strange, this "desert" country into which the southern boundary of Gogo loses itself. Possibilities as elusive as the desert itself may exist in that vast area, patches of good feed, a suspicion of latent growing powers in the soil, and the deepening conviction that water is obtainable by very shallow boring.

But the "desert" country of the great State is another and fascinating story, to be written only as daring and thoughtful men again and yet again push out into the grim lands. I have seen the bones of several of these, lying quiet as the solitude.

It is a strange, hateful country, this Australian desert: a few dream of its possibilities, some even return to probe its secrets further.

Northward, in the West Kimberleys, the cattle stations rapidly grow fewer until they peter out altogether not far north of the King Leopold Ranges. From here, right north to the cliffs of Cape Londonderry, facing a turbulent sea, is the wildman's country, where even yet he chips his stone spear heads, where even the craft of fashioning the axe of stone has not yet quite become extinct.

But the black man's numbers are much fewer than is popularly supposed. He is killing himself off, too, very rapidly, by an efficient method of birth-control. Disease is killing more; tribal feuds each year take their toll. Soon that wild country of craggy ranges, of hill and gorge and almost impenetrable coastline. will know him no more.

Very bravely, very strangely, too, when you see it at first hand, is the history of settlement being carried out along a fringe of the lower coast. Not more than half a dozen settlers, lands nearly inaccessible as yet other than by sea, growing peanuts - successfully, 2,000 miles from market. One of them even experimenting with sheep... Their communication

Top: Boabab tree, with its prehistoric forms. Below: Not far from Wyndham is the grave of the Head Stockman of *We of the Never Never*.

with the outside world a mission lugger... Stranger still, but very heartening in view of the almost complete absence of white women in the stations along the civilized portion of the West Kimberleys, these have their wives with them, and now children are coming. It is a cheery little object lesson - what a white man with his wife beside him is game enough to try to do, and to do under difficulties as great and in a land as inhospitable as any that our grandfathers pioneered 100 years ago.

The East Kimberleys, running as a strip from north to south, parallel with the Territory border, is more definitely settled. At its one port, Wyndham, landed the wanderers who fought their way south to the Kimberley goldfields, Hall's Creek. Great battling, 200 miles of valleys and hills defying their attempts to find a track... No wonder that that now historic way is paved with place-names that tell of struggles against those close-set ranges, those treacherous fording-places, those bogs and rocks and sands guarding No-man's-land. Here and there can still be seen grass-grown mounds, where men fell by the spears of the blacks. But cattle stations soon formed and spread east to link with the great runs across the Territory.

Westward, in the northern end of the East Kimberleys, the wild lands merge with the northern wilds of the West Kimberley. No whites here, except at the Forrest River mission.

The port for the West Kimberleys is little Derby, away down King Sound, where the Fitzroy empties into the muddy water. To here, every season, the cattle come from inland along the great Fitzroy Road. The mobs are shipped at Derby for Perth. Each beast costs approximately, from station to saleyard, £5 per head to ship and sell. This transport cost often leaves very little over for the grower. Occasionally, a pastoralist will have to send money to pay for freightage of his cattle when the market has realized less than £5 per head. As it has taken him four years to grow each beast, the experience is bitter. Wyndham, the port for the East Kimberleys, is away down at the end of Cambridge Gulf. Here, directly under the shadow of the Bastion Range, nestles quietly the tiny town. A mile further along the marsh edge, under the ramparts of the Bastion itself, is the meat-works. To here, every season, from the East Kimberleys, come the cattle to be turned, with amazing rapidity, into frozen and, now, chilled beef. Here call the ships from England. Would that far more ships called, for his land could fill twenty times those ships if only the meat market were found.

There are no sheep in the East Kimberleys, but half a dozen stations have prospered this year in the west. Those that are putting down bores, and otherwise helping Nature to help them, have every prospect of a prosperous future.

Grasses in the Kimberleys are peculiar to themselves. They and the lands will be developed to grow far more stock when population grows and the country is understandingly developed. At present, most stations are of 1,000,000 acres in extent. It requires more acres of land to run a beast in the Kimberleys than in the eastern States. Even so, the land cries for that thoughtful development which will increase its productive power, the first signs of which are already appearing with surprising and profitable results. A day will come when Kimberley lands will carry more homesteads than one to the million acres.

But to describe the Kimberleys in an article is beyond me. To attempt it is like flying over a country and imagining you understand all you have sped over below.

# 2

# Where The Wild Men Roam

*Experiences travelling North of the King Leopold Ranges in the Kimberleys, North-Western Australia*

A ROUGH camp this just a few branches leaning against a pandanus palm beside a native well! A shade, certainly, but no air of permanence. Yet there is an orderliness about these pack saddles placed evenly behind one another, with each halter, every strap in place; The pack-bags, too, except the tucker-bags, are strapped up ready, each pair by its saddle, all gear within reach. Just a swift swing up on to the back of horse and mule, and this little outfit could be moving within minutes. A small fire is burning with very little smoke. And no noisy bells on the animals feeding close by.

A rifle is leaning against the butt of a palm; beside it a man reclines, smoke drifting lazily up from his pipe. He is a small man with wrinkled forehead and small, hard grey eyes. There is an alertness about those eyes, initiative around that tight-shut mouth, the tan of changing seasons upon his grizzled cheeks. An open flannel above riding trousers clothes a body of whip-cord and sinew. The thumb of his lean brown hand is tucked just behind the revolver holster at his belt.

A black-gin bends over the fire, a shrewd determined-looking woman of the wilds. Quite evidently she sticks by her white lord because she wants to; she likes him; she bosses him, too, to his surly acquiescence. An air of the tiger-cat about her pairs well with the watchful readiness of

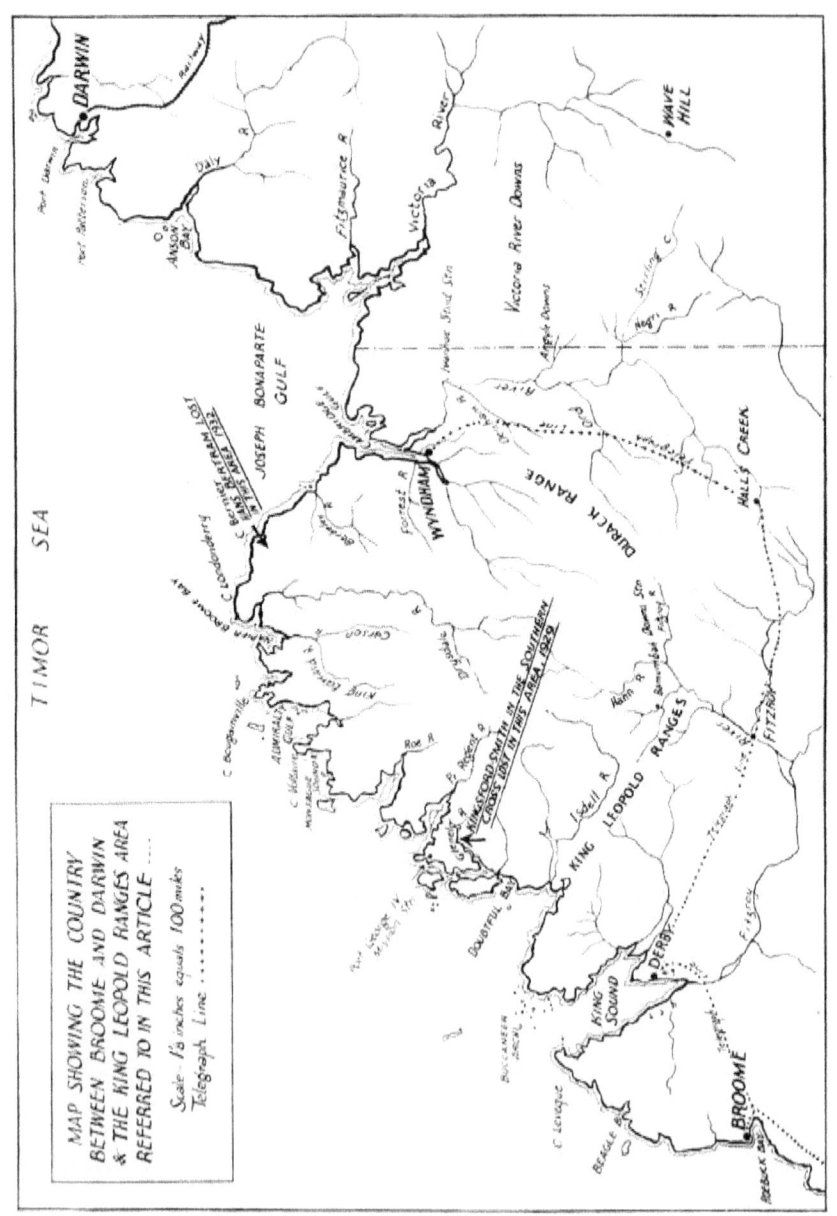

her mate. A cattle-dog near by with prick-eared watchfulness gazes at the mules and horses feeding amongst the timber. A wide-awake camp, this.

They saw us first, though our blackboys had smelt their fire even before they heard our horses' hoofs. They just gazed silently as we rode up. Greetings established just what we were and who we were, then followed the invitation to unpack and have a drink of tea.

A dingo-poisoner's camp this, far north of the King Leopolds, in the last strongholds of the Kimberley wild lands (only a long corner strip of the Kimberleys is wild now.) A few months ago, wild dog scalps were worth £2 apiece in Western Australia. But very few "doggers" indeed penetrated to such a locality as this.

We told him where we had seen the last dog-tracks in the sands of a waterhole in a deep gorge away back in the ranges. We mentioned nigger tracks too. In return he told us of good feed and water ahead. "You'll find two of my horses there," he added grimly, "full of shovel-nosed spears." We nodded to the implied caution.

A type, these men, professional hunters of the wild dog. Just a few of them; generally each roams his "own country" just as a black tribe roams theirs. This wizened little battler before us won our cautious respect. A first-class bushman in the true meaning of the word, he could well look after himself in all this isolation, whether against the forces of Nature, the blacks, or white men as tough as himself. Just occasionally out there circumstances force a man to become a law unto himself. This chap had recently shot a white man, accidentally, of course. The bullet grazed the jugular vein; but the man leaped out into the night to survive. They breed 'em tough over there.

It was many days before we met another white man. Of all things in the world he was driving a string of camels. No wonder our horses went mad; the pack mules simply took to the bush. Camels! out here in the mountains!

He laughed uproariously while we scoured the bush for our vanished mules. We could hear the animals breaking through the timber, hear his laugh growing fainter behind us. But he was a likeable chap, a merry bushman this, and that night he just talked and talked while we laughed. To hear him one would have thought that pioneering was just one joke after another.

He had not seen a white man for many months. Perhaps the solitude made him think more. Anyway, he had solved his transport problem. It looked impossible, and in fact his country is vaguely mapped "inaccessible."

Impossible to get wheeled transport in over the ranges; no landing ground for a 'plane, and none to land; while pack horse transport could carry only the lightest of loads. So he brought a string of camels from 500 miles away, and further- more found a: pad for them over rocky country. He had turned the ships of the desert into ships of the mountains to carry his produce to the coast, where a tiny lugger took it on the first stage of its voyage to the market 2,000 miles away.

A pioneer, in modern days. There are just a few such, creeping out into the last of the wild lands, their all on a string of pack-horses and mules. Sometimes two will travel prospecting for country in company; sometimes one will go alone, travelling in the big loneliness until he comes on some little pocket of good land. This he gazes on, the site of his future home. Building the bark bumpy from the paper-barks near by he takes his requirements from the land, making it keep him. In twenty years that land will probably be settled, and those few isolated men and women will be the "old pioneers."

A difficult country to pioneer, for lines of ranges rise as walls to bar travel from north to south; and local peculiarities in the grasses complicate choice of land. The grassy valleys may look lovely during four months of the year, but be hungry and parched in the dry season; or the green of the lowlands may prove deceptive and sour. The black soil may

Top: A North Australian policeman crosses a river on a paperbark raft, aided by two Aboriginal trackers.
Below: An Aboriginal family group on a Kimberely pastoral station, 1890.

not be truly black, the Mitchell and Flinders grasses may not be the true grasses. A man has to learn his waters and herbage as well as his country. He has to solve his own transport problem, be his own doctor, do and build everything on his own initiative, and with his own hands, solve that market problem, and laugh at the loneliness. And a man who laughs at loneliness is brave indeed. If he fails, he fails alone; he "walks out" with what horses have not fallen to poison weed or spears; he leaves behind him, too, a few years of his life. Lucky, indeed, if he can leave behind him the bitterness of heart.

A wild, inhospitable corner of the continent this; apparently it will defy settlement to the last. Its treacherous coastline of a thousand bays, a thousand islands, a thousand capes; its roaring tides, its whirlpools and erratic currents lashing its barren cliffs - all these seem to defy penetration from the sea, while from the air it looks a nightmare.

So it is only the toughest of men who roam its fastnesses. None at all in its farthest north, only a police patrol when a Bertram comes crash or some wandering Ulysses of the sea is buffeted by Nature or by natives. South of the Prince Regent is an occasional wanderer, who to live must understand the bush in both its wet season and its dry, who must find his way about a wilderness that knows no single road. He must understand the black man in his own land, he must have learned how to snatch a living out of that land, and how to return to some outpost when needs must.

Among these dozen or so of nomads are two outstanding on land, several also on sea. For the entire coast of the North is home to wanderers who in their tiny craft poke in here and there and God knows where, and earn a living similarly. But the two landsmen mentioned of this particular corner are without plant, owning no horses or mules or camels. Each travels alone, on foot, taking to the bush with a rifle, a blanket, a knife, and matches. They are really men who lived a thousand years ago and have not yet been reborn into modern life. I have met their type in the

Gulf country, and in the jungle areas of North Queensland. They fear not man nor insect, snake nor crocodile nor fever. They live on the rifle, by their knowledge of the wildfowl life of the lagoons and billabongs, of the fish in creek or river. They have lived among the blacks and learned of the plant food of the bush, how to find and prepare and cook it. They sleep in a trench scooped in the sand, or on a grass couch under an overhanging rock, or on the fallen leave that they heap up between the protecting flanges of some giant tree. Their legs develop the sinews of the black man, their hearing and sight are almost as keen as his, their endurance develops similarly. Safety demands friendship, or strict neutrality with the blacks.

Yet even these men vary in degree. I have known of two who scorned the tribesmen whenever they met a wandering band, who considered themselves the very kings of the wild. One of these is a huge chap, who stalks through the bush with the noiseless and tireless tread of a panther, a rifle in his hand, a knife at his belt, wild eyes glaring above a big red beard. Yet among the blacks of the north there are warriors as powerful, as aggressive, fiercer even than he. A little while back he strode into a big camp where there was a number of such warriors, who had gathered, too, for the ceremony of the Rising Moon. He fought his way out. His physical strength is a byword. He needed the ferocity of a tiger with it now, for he was almost chopped to pieces by tomahawks. He crawled to his lair like a wounded animal, he licked his wounds, then plastered them with clay and feathers and ashes; and he battled his way right back to civilization. Now he is again wandering the wilds.

We wondered, out there in the great Isdell Gorge, whether he still has his nerve. It is a priceless thing to those who do not abuse its power, the indefinable thing we call nerve, that enables a man to stride fearlessly and even happily into danger from which many of us would quail.

But the sickening chops of a tomahawk can break the stoutest nerve.

Map showing Arnhem Land, which is approximately the size of England.

# 3

# Arnhem Land

I enjoyed a yarn yesterday with probably the last of the old-time explorers - Larry Wells, seventy-five years young, straight as a gun barrel, his eyes keen above a short grey moustache. It was Wells who in 1896 travelled from south to north up through the Westralian desert area, beating Carnegie to the Fitzroy by a fortnight. They faced unknown country, hundreds of miles of waterless tracts; but they butted through with camel transport alone. Tough men! Young Carnegie went to Africa and continued exploring until a pygmy's poisoned arrow sent him across the Great Divide. Wells at seventy-five still carries on; recently he walked a thirty-mile Centralian dry stage, but these days his jobs are in country that has been "gone over."

"Show me a spot anywhere in Australia where no white man has been within fifty miles of it," he invited me.

Very nearly true; such spots are difficult to find. Still, there are a few, and even bigger "spots." One of the biggest remaining is Arnhem Land. On the Northern Territory map it is a large vacant space east of Darwin, on which neither station nor field is marked. A few undecided lines represent waterways whose course is problematical, while the few ranges represented are mostly guesswork. On the large scale maps the country is mostly a series of blanks.

This is the real Arnhem Land, not the settled Roper Valley lands fringing it to the south, which more and more frequently are alluded to as Arnhem Land.

There are no explorers' routes criss-crossing this area of the map. But, even so, white men have trod its solitudes in places. Mostly long-distance police patrols from Darwin, engaged in that apparently impossible job of finding and arresting native killers along the banks of the Alligator River, and the buffalo-shooters have ridden well into the fringe. Old Dr. Bloomfield. of Darwin, with blacks as companions, recently penetrated a considerable distance into this wild country, and his sketch plan of the route, now being worked on by the Government map-men in Darwin, will mark one definite little track.

A great "character," the old doctor; a wanderer in the strange places of many lands, he owed his nine lives to his knowledge of medicine and his ready wit in taking advantage of the superstitions in the native mind.

But the Australian bush is a hard mistress. No man can put the witch-doctor business over her. This was the doctor's last trip. A sick man, he shipped from Darwin, only to die recently in Brisbane.

One lone old prospector, Billy Alderson, also penetrates into one particular area of the country, slave to the call of gold. An interesting character, he has seen the young natives go, scattered tribal hordes grow up to initiation and warriorhood. He knows hundreds of them by tribal name, knows their loves and hopes, their hates and passions. He knows the killers among them, and holds the secrets of many a grim feud and tragedy, and even knows their Mali, their spirit people; he knows the dread secret of Ragalk. Master of numerous "lingos," he has passed unharmed among the natives for over thirty years. He rarely wears a shirt, always travels "light," and thus can travel fast should necessity arise. His book of life is the ever-changing book of crag and scrub and plain, of lagoon and unmapped waterway, of signal smokes and the vendettas of savage men. Above all he knows how to mind his own business. In this fascinating book of his, he turns over a few pages occasionally when he travels into country he has never seen before. If only he had some slight

Native Policeman with his trackers and their families, Arnhem Land, 1930.

Aboriginals supporting a mule train in Arnhem Land, with their "find", an extremely long snake.

slight knowledge of surveying he could have mapped a fair portion of this land.

The many twists and turns of the Arnhem Land coastline are heavily wooded mostly with low species of timber, specked with beaches and sandhills. Spreading salt arms fringed with man- groves run inland, their waters the haunt of the crocodile. The paper-bark swamps, whose white-coated trees, often beautiful, rise from stagnant depths of yellow water, are lily-covered. Further inland are plains, generally scrub-entangled, coarsely grassed. Numbers of these low-lying areas become lagoons, and, in the boggy places, quagmires after the wet season. Still farther inland are the ranges, generally fairly low, and covered by "bush" timber; occasionally though, the ranges are picturesque. One such, seen for the first time, was gone through recently by a venturesome police patrol travelling through Loololl-pool-pool-e to the native lagoon Merra-coola. North-east of here they passed through broken country into a castellated sandstone range with huge pillars towering skyward. With the horses picking their way through fallen boulders, they travelled the valley for miles, imagining that the crumbled walls on either side were the relics of a ruined city. They named it the Ruined City and were surprised to learn, when the trackers questioned a band of nomads, that the native name was, as closely as their meaning could approximate, the "Ruined City." In ages gone by it had been the meeting place of the "great camps." Still visible were the shrub - overgrown relics of their stone "sacred places." One of the mounted men in this particular patrol dabbles a little in sketching, and it is hoped that his pencilled sketches will help to fill in a little of the map hereabouts.

Four or five missions cling to the island system of the coast, or are situated up one or another of the rivers. Perhaps the most interesting surroundings of these is Oenpelli, on the East Alligator River over the fringe of Arnhem Land. Away from the river is a range, picturesque in its cliffs and bastions and escarpments of battlemented rock. One big "split" hill looks as if it has been rent asunder by some terrible upheaval. Near by is a native burial ground and not far away an armoury, both the catacombs and the industry of tribes stretching far away back through the ages. A man could get lost in those breakages among the rocks just as the history of the vanished tribes is lost. Upon cleft after cleft are the bones-bones of the ages, all colours, skulls that have been grinning there for many, many. years. Much older are those stained, musty heaps of powder, long grown over by shrubs of prickly bush that had died and lived again season after season. At the armoury lie many heaps of chipped stone in all stages of chipping, and flakings where stone tomahawks, daggers and initiation knives and spear-heads have been prepared for war and the hunt. Among the boulders and on long bare shelves of flat rock lie heaps of axe-heads discarded in the finishing process because of some last minute flaws in the flint; near by in a heap of half-finished heads discarded earlier, there are numerous fragments and chips and flakings. Here and there lie heaps of stone brought up in the rough; a few selected stones are ready laid aside.

With the exception of the border mission stations, no whites live in Arnhem Land proper; it is still the home of our stone age man. Only the Creator knows for how many years, probably many tens of thousands of years, the aboriginal has lived and died there and still lives as a relic of long past human history. He is a rather warlike aboriginal, too, especially the native of the coastal tribes. And most of the victories have been on his side. During this last twenty years his little list of killings is quite surprising. He killed even Campbell, that elusive character by land and sea, whom some of the best bushmen police in the world could not catch. His list of luggers looted and burned at the water's edge makes quite a respectable tally in the annals of canoe piracy. Probably what has helped to make him so bold is the admixture of Malay blood, for the proas of these sea-raiders have, until recent years, visited our northern shores for centuries past. Pearl shell and trepang were the lures, and the right royal fights waged upon those savage shores in times gone by have come down to the young aboriginal in corroboree and legend.

Unfortunately, the Malay left something else behind him with the admixture of his virile blood, something to counteract it in the form of venereal disease, while Chinese wanderers left their taint in leprosy. The white man receives continent-wide blame for the first-named scourge, but he has never been in this land, not in numbers.

Arnhem Land will be a wild-man's land for years to come, perhaps many years. Perhaps it may remain a living museum of stone-age animals and birds and reptiles until the last of the Balamoomoos have passed away.

Darwin harbour 1935, with the SS *Marella* on the ocean side, and the Australian Survey ship, the HMAS *Morseby*, nearside.

# 4

# Darwin, North Australia

DARWIN is pretty and busy in this summer day of '35.

It has a fine harbour, ringed by little wooded cliffs, which some day will be rich with peeping bungalows. The foundation is there, for on shore, high over the funnel of the Marella, are well-known roofs above the bamboos, the shrubs, and the palms, while away back along the broad, bush-clad roads are signs of building activity that augur well for the spread of the town.

The weekly train from the back country has just arrived with a load of mining men and optimism. For there is a mild boom in the Territory's minerals. Several treatment plants are working, and the results will decide whether the boom has come to stay.

A movement of cars and trucks gives a business-like air to the town; loads of station stores are going down to the railway; a military lorry loaded with soldiers rumbles by. In the town centre, men dressed in cool whites walk with that jaunty air which indicates that business is "looking up." Occasionally a white woman steps by, and her freshness is a tribute to the climate. So are the singing voices of the children, nearly lifting the school roof. A little crowd of coloured men stand gazing at the placards outside the local talkies. That aristocrat among natives, a tracker in uniform, is pointing with disdain to the over-saddled horse from which the cowboy hero is portrayed as firing guns and lassooing villains all at once.

"Me no more dam fool!" declares the tracker, scornfully; "no more catchem man that way! Gib us plurry laugh."

For a time at least, the unemployed at Darwin have got work. The big aerodrome is busy, the wireless station and the bond store are building, while the Marella has just landed a thousand tons of cargo, mining machinery mostly. If only some of the mines prove payable, Darwin will not look back. There is plenty to talk about. Darwin is now the port for the overseas air mail, and newspaper men from the big southern press are stationed here. The native question which so keenly touches everyone in the Territory makes names such as Nemarluk, Tuckiar, Tiger, Muderitch, "Longlegs," Wongo, "Butcher," and half a dozen others familiar to everyone. While people down south generally connect these names with the murders of Japanese fishermen, the whites here connect them with the murder of white men. The south is far away; people see the picture only dimly. But up here, when men fall to the shovel-nosed spears, people feel the shock right at home.

See that man passing the Commercial Bank, that lithely-built chap walking so deceptively slowly? He is a buffalo shooter from the Adelaide River, a thousand-a-year-man. Each year he ships that number of hides. A little while back they were worth £2/10/- a hide; now they are hardly worth getting. This man is one of the Buffalo Bills of the North, his life one romantic chapter after another. Crocodile, buffalo, wild native, fire and floods on land, storms at sea-all come into the picture of his life.

The buffalo shooters solve their transport problem both by sea and by land. Some own a lugger, which brings their stores from Darwin to a coastal camp, while men inland use trucks for overland transportation to the nearest point on the railway. As is common in the Territory, they make their own roads, going straight "bush" to come back on their tracks, until, after a few trips, the wheels beat down a road. It is rough on the trucks, numbers of which bear evidence of crude but effective bush

Aviatrix Amy Johnson (sitting left) and group on her arrival in Darwin, 1930.

Chinese procession along the main streets of Darwin, 1916.

engineering. A man has to understand his job thoroughly and possess wide bush experience and initiative to make a success of buffalo shooting. He must understand the handling of many horses and natives, organize transportation and the quick movements of his camps, and know the changing difficulties of his far-flung country both in the wet and in the dry.

In portions of the Territory, the slate-grey herds roam the plains as in those stories of the prairies we associate with our Red Indian schoolboy days. But in real life the scene is shifted; the buffalo herds in truth roam the wild Northern Australian plains, but the American prairies no more.

See that tall chap over there, the one whose new whites emphasize the weather tan on his face? Can you recognize the walk of a horseman? He has just come in after a 500-mile trip out Victoria River way. He manages a station larger than England. The Fitzmaurice River blacks raid his cattle fairly often, and have threatened to spear him, too. His travel mileage per year is enormous; his droving days are dangerous, too, with the fording of waterways against current, snag, crocodile, bog, and treacherously shifting sand. His cattle roam over thousands of square miles of wild bush; his stockmen ride with a gun at their belt.

Here comes a totally different type - big, broad shouldered, the unmistakable roll of the sea in his walk. Clear blue eyes in a strongly-cut face. This is the Skipper, master of a pearling fleet. His experiences of the pearling seas, of adventure with Japanese, Malay, Koepanger and Black would fill half a dozen books. He has looked on famous pearls, some with an eventful history; he has worked at the bottom of the sea as well as on the surface. His great swim from the wreck of a pearling during the famous hurricane is a story known to all the fleets of the Coral Seas.

With half-a-dozen townsmen he invades the Victoria Hotel. The Darwin pearlers are content, for the newly-discovered pearl-shell beds are turning out wonderfully well, and the fleet is "all in" for the catch of the season. Up against a very low price for shell and the menace of the Japanese fishers in most modern craft, the Darwin men have put their shoulder - the wheel. Modern gear, fresh methods, and work. Results already attained augur well for a prosperous year.

Right from here we see a pretty craft just skimming to anchorage - white-painted, smart, swift. We can faintly hear. the rattle of the chain as overboard goes the mud-hook. Now her owner comes ashore. A sea roamer this, of that interesting type brought about by the War and the ever-changing circumstances of life. He was a companion flier of Kingsford Smith's in his battling days and, in the crazy machines of the war his exploits ranked high in the annals of flying. Now he roams the Arafura and the Timor, a freelance of the sea. I will not repeat his boarding of the Malay proas trespassing in Australian waters and the adventures resulting from that highly colourful episode, for in a sketchy way they have already been "written up."

So we stroll down Kavenagh Street, lined with its Chinese shops, dingy places mostly. A European touch is given by half a dozen motor cars parked under the big banyan tree. There is no bustling business about this Chinatown, bur there distinct air that "any old day will do." The inhabitants have plenty of time to talk, and we hear chem chatter as we pass shop after shop, though in the dim recesses of some we catch a glimpse of men and women toiling silently over ironing boards. On the doorsteps of some of the shops, people with that shifty stare, sit to watch us pass. Old Celestials sit there, too, their locks scanty and grey, dull blotches on their nearly bald craniums.

From a more prosperous-looking shop, a Chinese girl looks out; she has that expression which tells she sees us, yet doesn't see us, and is not interested anyway. She is dressed modernly, is solemn of feature, with staring brown eyes, but has grown the slim figure and independent ·walk that comes with breeding under Australian skies.

A little woman in blue pants and long black coat-gown clatters past on wooden shoes. No hat, long, black hair brushed severely back. Half-a-dozen big-eyed youngsters cling to her pants or trot along behind. Chinatown knows no birth-control, and the problem of alien increase is not to be disregarded. Darker-coloured people here and there drift in and out of the shops; there is an odd white about, enterprise looks dead. Yet several of these stores must do business, for some are well stocked. Several pretty coloured girls pass by with laughing chatter, a timid boldness about their stare. The lighter-skinned of the different mixtures. are well dressed and quite conscious of their good figures.

We turn sharply to the right along a "white" street leading towards the Residency. To our left, through the trees, we get glimpses of the blue waters of the harbour. Distantly across is Talc Head, where Nemarluk turned at bay, defeated the trackers, and again escaped. We pass the long, white building of the Government offices, and catch a glimpse of men smartly dressed in khaki shirts and trousers, and wearing broad-brimmed hats - men of the Northern Territory Mounted Police, whose thousand-mile patrols vie with the best work of the Canadian Mounted.

Yes, Darwin is interesting at present; it will come definitely on the map, provided the old mines now being equipped with machinery turn out gold.

# 5

# West Of The Darling

MENINDEE looks pretty at dawn, when silvering rays come slanting between the gums upon the river. Way down there, within the steep black banks, is the "Oscar W." emerging from the form of a shadow ship. Captain Ron. Johnson is up on the quaint little bridge, hardly distinguishable as he supervises the crew hauling on the big rope hawsers tied to trees. A burly figure moves among them, Captain Lance Maclean, surely one of the strongest men on the river. He has carried several bales of sheepskins up the steep-set plank to the bank. Each bale weighs five and a half hundredweight. It takes all the strength of an ordinary man to lift and walk away with one hundredweight.

With a churning of the paddle-wheel the craft gets under way while yet the sharp bends of the river arc a shadowed mystery. She tows a big iron barge, which when tired up with three hundred tons of wool appears as if gliding through the old gum-branches.

In the opening up of this country many famous "Darling Dreadnoughts" did their share; but the advent of the motor has driven them off the river, as steam has driven the sailing ships from the sea.

Dawn shows Menindee in another light - a scattered little Township of brick houses and less pretentious ones of iron, ominous sand mounds piling up against some of the yards. It is almost level country, with a red sandhill here and there. there are scattered clumps of mulga trees, and the dull blue-grey of blue-bush. It looks a hot, dusty place, and often is so. There is an atmosphere as of livelier days around it though, and, curiously enough, one hears talk of Burke and Wills as if they had passed through but a month or so ago. For this country is rich in marked trees and in place-names of the ill-fated explorers. Their memory is still green.

A tall, thin old chap is working with the dawn. "Is it true you never sleep?" I asked with a smile.

"I can't make money while I sleep," he replied, and measured me with that steady glance of his. He is Jack Cleary, who saw the old coach days go out, and who drove the first motor mail in Australia. He saw, too, a Darling Dreadnought go cruising forty miles overland in the big flood of 1870.

My trip this time was west of the Darling, to the Queensland and South Australian border. There is no glamour of new country in such a trip. But it is an object-lesson, which teaches much and leaves room for troubled thought. For, apparently, the country is slipping backward; it is not the same land that the pioneers knew. Instead of plains alternating with gentle rises, flowering under herbage and saltbush, mulga and gidyea, it is now almost bare over certain areas, wind-swept and sandy. True, the last five years have seen no general heavy downpour of rain. Still, the stations carry barely half the herds that made this area so prosperous in ·the pioneer days. Numerous "permanent" water-holes over a big stretch of country are now completely silted up. Overstocking, and particularly the recurring rabbit plagues, are held mainly responsible.

Millions of sheep, hundreds of thousands of cattle feeding for fifty years ate much of the herbage to the roots. Great quantities, too, of seed were eaten. Then came the plagues of rabbits, and these ate not only the roots of plants but even ring- barked the edible shrubs and trees. When this plague does come, some stations poison as many as 10,000 rabbits around one tank in a single night. I have seen the rabbit hosts by day so thick that the country looked like a moving carpet. This, in a country of low rainfall, spells disaster. When the storms did come, the

Top: Remnants of an old coach on the Strzelecki track.
Below: Type of country north of Lake Frome.

downpours cut into the slopes, loosening the top sail, which was washed into the creeks. The surface of the country, no longer bound together by grass and roots of shrub and plant, was whirled up by the winds and blown in dust away.

In the course of time many of the pioneers' water-holes have been silted up, while the wind in places has blown the top soil away and left claypans like bare red scars upon the earth. Not a pretty picture, but it is there! Stations and selectors carry on with the hope that a good cycle must come again. A few recurring good seasons and the country will bloom anew.

It is food for thought, too, that forty years ago this country gave employment to far greater numbers than it does to-day, and that the now quiet bush towns (some are quite dead) were once thriving and busy. The fading of small goldfields and the dwindling of the stock the country carries are partly responsible for this. Also, forty years ago and more, the country was being developed. Every station employed its team of tank and well-sinkers, its fencers, teamsters, homestead builders, and station hands. Now all that work is over. Stations that once employed sixty men get along at present with ten.

Then came motor transport, which had and is having a vast influence in the destiny of Australia. Before the car came, there were numerous bush roads west of the Darling, and over all of these rose the dust-cloud of road transport, and came the creak of heavy wheels. Many teamsters had loaded with rations and lumbered along to station and town, returning to the river to unload their wool on the "Dreadnoughts." There were drays and carts and buggies and buckboards; the mail coach with its unbroken colts plunging to break the record and the harness, too; horse and bullock-teams, camel-teams, pack-teams. Drovers' turnouts were on every road. Hundreds of saddlers, harness-makers, wheelwrights, blacksmiths, all found plentiful work. Now all these are gone.

Motor transport will shift a wool clip in a fortnight that would have taken teams months to cart away. Journeys of a day used to take a week, and a hard week, too. Motor-cars are used even to go around the paddocks on occasion, and a man can now make in one day on inspection of stock that previously would have necessitated his riding from sunset to dark, and camping out for five or six nights. Nearly all the shepherds and many boundary riders have gone. Whereas the dray and horse team used to take four days to cart rations to an out camp, the station lorry now does it in half a day, saving the up-keep of horses in dry times besides. The installation of bush telephones to out-stations has also dispensed with considerable horse-work, saving much time also.

Yet, perversely enough, motor transport has proved a blessing. though it has put many out of work, still many a station in these drier area parts could not now keep going were it not for the cheaper, quicker, and time-saving motor. Continued dry times, low prices for cattle and wool, the lessened carrying capacity of the country, would have made it unprofitable to carry on. It is an interesting study this country west of the Darling. It has passed through the pioneer stage, the development stage, the producing stage. It is still in the producing stage; but Time has brought unexpected problems for man to cope with, and the fight is to be staged all over again.

This "West of the Darling" was essentially the bush of Henry Lawson. But it is fast developing, and a change is gradually coming into the manner of life of the humans living therein. The old order has almost completely changed in the last twenty-five years. Gone are the wayside shanties; only a crumbling chimney, a pepper tree, and a heap of bottles now mark a hundred places once lively with the sprees, the dances, the race meetings of twenty years ago. Gone, too, are the "characters" once known on every road, at every station, in every township. Gone, also, are the professional swagmen, though their place is momentarily taken by the inexperienced victims of the depression. Gone are the days of the spanking turnouts of six-in-hand, flying to catch a special train. Strange thought that the squatter of those days and the swagmen of those days should be passing out together! The change is very noticeable, too in the absence of the travelling crowds of shearers and rouse-shearing within a few hours, and are moving again an hour or two after the shed cuts out. When the season is over, they travel swiftly to the nearest railway, and are soon speeding to the cities, there to spend their time and money until shearing starts again. That is another phase of motor transport: money whirls past the tiny townships, instead of staying as in the brave days of the horse. This change has almost entirely eliminated the bush "hard-cases." You cannot be a "character" when everybody is going somewhere, for no one has time to listen. The tendency, too, is more and more towards specialized labour, ready to move quickly from place to place as wanted. In such ever-shifting scenes, Hellfire Jack, Scandalous Graham, Tim the Rager, Harry the Nark, Barefoot Jimmy, Kelly the Rake, and others of the carefree fraternity find little opportunity to develop their talents.

Yes, west of the Darling both country and men are changing. It must be so, as nothing stays still. Some prophesy that, in another thirty years, that country will stand use only as "shepherding" country after a good season, that the oncoming Sand Fiend will cripple it.

But perhaps Man will defy both Wind and Sand by some mighty irrigation scheme from the Darling.

# 6

# Sand

*Impressions of a large tract of dry country in the interior of Australia*

AN INTRIGUING country, touched by desolation, tinged by richness; floor of a long-dead sea; alternating between desert and pasture land; changeable as its winds, uncertain as its shifting sands; at one season a complete desert, at another a source of supply to clouds that may water Central Australia.

In a continent it is but a small area, but it is big for all that. Approximately four hundred miles from north to south, and nearly as broad, it spreads over portion of South Australia, follows the Simpson Desert north into the Territory, and stretches east across the south-western border of Queensland, just tipping over into the north-west corner of New South Wales.

An area blessed by glorious winters, harsh summers! Its timbers are so sparse that a big tree is a jewel. Its bird life is elusive, until the flood-birds come in myriads before the oncoming waters, only like them to vanish.

It is the area that some old-time explorer called the "Dead Heart." He saw it in drought, when it really was "dead," a vast expanse of gibber plains, stretching hot and dry to end in shimmering mirage-a desolation of sand-ridges under a pitiless sun, swimming in a terrible loneliness. One can ride day after day in the isolation of these ridges and believe himself in the heart of the Arabian Desert, but never in Australia. Yet, with an ordinary sparse rainfall, herbage springs up on the needle-wood flats, and the sandhills blossom yellow, scarlet, and purple under desert flowers.

It is our land of the night-parrot, of the burrowing mole, of the sightless snake, of things so elusive that they are no more than a hiss or a squeak in the night. Even so, only one section of this harsh area has successfully defied the white man-the Simpson Desert. Much of the rest of it he has exploited for sixty years because it has grown scanty but sweet grasses, which quickly fatten his herds.

The secret of it lies in the great lakes system - grim Lake Eyre, Lake Torrens, and the chain of salt lakes that runs through the north of South Australia. These are the big fellows; there are smaller ones in south-west Queensland and the north-west corner of New South Wales. The smaller are unnoticeable things, seldom carrying water; yet they illustrate the laws of cause and effect which dominate the entire continent. These shallow depressions point with withered hands to pages from the past-a mighty past, when Central Australia had its inland sea of sweet water fed by great rivers from the north, when the now bare red earth was covered by the green· of forests, when herds of diprotodons lumbered over the plains, and giant kangaroos clawed the tree-branches. We find their bones now in Lake Calabonna, the bones, too, of other creatures mightier still, in almost all the "dead lakes."

What cataclysms, or what slow changes in temperature and climate, converted this luxuriance into semi-desert we can only surmise. But as a nation we should awaken to the fact that in this locality another change is now taking place with alarming rapidity: the "dead heart" is fast turning into a "creeping desert." And with the winds it is drifting down towards our good lands, the lands that feed our cities.

I would hate to be an alarmist; but then I have the eyes to see things, and, when men of wider experience than mine, men who have lived a lifetime on the borders of that country, say emphatically that their better lands will be desert in twenty years, then it is time indeed for a voice to cry in the wilderness.

Already stations have been overwhelmed by sand, even townships now are threatened. Towards where the sand is drifting, stations that thirty years ago sheared 100,000 sheep are now lucky to shear 40,000. Cattle-stations that fed 6,000 head are now hard pressed to feed 2,000

Man has upset the balance of Nature. Upon this sparse rain-fall country, he has for sixty years grazed many millions of cattle and sheep. In an area of very poor timber resources, he has used the axe unsparingly. Plagues of rabbits in teeming millions have followed him. These and sheep have not only eaten the herbage but the very roots of the bushes, have even ringbarked the trees. Thus the binding of roots that held the sand-hills together has gone. The seasonal winds blow strongly as ever, but they carry the sand-the drifting sand.

It is a great problem, which shortly will have to be thought about nationally. Let us go back to the dry salt lakes.

Unfortunately dry! Many years ago, when seasonally they were filled, or nearly so, they provided shallow but vast sheets of water upon which beat a fierce sun. Evaporation formed thunder clouds, which, blown away by the winds, fell as storms over inland Australia. To-day, the same winds blow, but they carry sand-drift instead of raindrops.

The lakes are not now filled, because the arteries that carried the flood-water into them are now partly choked up. There are three main arteries - the Georgina, the Diamantina, and the Cooper. Many seasons ago, when heavy rain would fall in Northern Australia, these three great meandering watercourses would roll down right through from Western Queensland, roll on through the sand-ridges in northern South Australia, and eventually spill their yellow waters into the lakes. The Finke, in Central Australia, acted similarly, but in much lesser degree.

The arteries are choked up in numerous places mainly through soil erosion. Here again Man has upset the balance of Nature.

Even though hundreds of miles from the arid area, the inevitable law still holds. It works to a similar result even through different

Top: The author C.T. Madigan crossing the 'Dead Heart.'
Bottom: An Aboriginal elder sand drawing, Haast's Bluff.

agencies - the axe, over-stocking. Hence the loosened soil. The seasonal rains that come in this more northern area wash this loosened soil from the hills and flats into the creeks, whence it is carried to the river-beds and deposited. Not noticeably at first, but after sixty years very much so. Many thousands of tons of silt have been washed into those old river-beds, which traverse hundreds of miles of flat country. The river-beds in paces slowly but surely begin to choke up. The floods come. The water is blocked, it spills out over the bank, and spreads over the flat areas, returning by many channels to the old bed. Bur again it is blocked, and again and again and again. The result is that very little, if any, of the flood water now reaches the old lake basins. Hence the lakes are becoming "dead" indeed; they do not secure the water without which there is no evaporation to help the arid country with thunder-storms.

It looks as if man will have to take all the stock off that country for a period of years and "spell" it, thus giving its remnant of bush life a chance to build up again and spread and once more grip the sand, will need to do the same even farther north to give the grasses a chance to grow again and carpet the earth against soil erosion. If we do not do something like this, it really looks as if the prophecy of the old hands out there will come true. That area will turn into desert. Worse still, its drifting sands will then creep all the faster down upon us.

Nature offers us a book of simple but wonderful lessons, which we learn only by long and often bitter experience. She takes her time; so we forget lesson after lesson, until the disastrous cumulative one comes along. She shows us cause and effect, worthy of our serious study. She is Fire, a benevolent and helpful servant. She is perfect in herself; it is we who make the mistakes. In her arid areas her scanty grasses and bushes are marvels of life battling against environment; through the ages they have developed properties that make them probably the best drought-resisting grasses in the world - and the sweetest. For stock will thrive and fatten on those semi-desert plants more quickly than on the "softer" grasses of the well-watered coast. But those grasses are far er to replace than coastal grasses. And here a secret.

Nature whispers to us that we are killing our grasses by burning "both ends of the candle." The grasses "shelter" moisture; they actually conserve it in more ways than one. We overstock and not only eat away the grass but leave the earth bare; thus the moisture in it, unprotected by shade, is rapidly dried up by the sun, and the soil blows away in dust. Many lessons,we also we take so long to learn. And the grass and bush of the arid regions is so thinly placed that it is all eaten up while we are learning.

Perhaps it is hard to understand from our homes in the cities, or from our sheltered farm or station on the coastal lands. But "out there" you can see once solid hills now sticking up like the decayed teeth of old men, the broken fragments of hills blown away in dust.

Nature teaches us of soil erosion, too, that not only does it affect the direct locality denuded, but in this case it affects us hundreds of miles away, in our arid country.

For, years ago, when the floods used to come down into the great lakes, the country would blossom like the rose, even though rain had not fallen on it for years. The flooding of the lands as the rivers swept by did that. But now that soil erosion, even though in the far north, blocks the waters from coming to the Centre, well-the sand-drift is travelling towards our south.

It is a long line, many hundreds of miles of cause and effect. From the watersheds of the farthest north of North Australia right down deep into South Australia, into south-western Queensland, and now creeping into north-west New South Wales. But there it is.

Cause and effect, change and counter-change, over a huge area. What we may be forced to think of is whether this change in the arid regions will ultimately affect us right away down south and south-east !

It is not a pleasant subject, but we have warnings from the dead ages to guide us. We know that several of the great deserts of the old lands were once thickly populated, that forests grew there and great fields of grasses. We have learned this of late years by the excavations that have shown us not only the bones of animals, birds, and fishes, but also the ruins of old cities long since buried under the sands. What, then, changed those once populous lands into deserts so dire that even the memory of their populations has been buried under the sand? Does history repeat itself?

Hence, if a few good seasons come and still this drifting sand comes creeping towards us, we should do something - speedily.

Drought hits the Darling River in our Federation year.

Taking crocodiles on the Daly River, 1933.

# 7

# Lazy Days In Crocodile Land

IT'S a glorious day. The *Swanee* is sailing like a dream. Blue sky, blue sea, gulls lazily circling, while porpoises frolic within feet of the gently-moving bows! Up forward the aboriginal crew lie sprawled on deck, the sun warming their shining bodies. Hermann sits aft mending a sail, while the "Pirate" stands by the tiller commiseratingly eyeing the snoring natives. "Poor, downtrodden slaves!" he sighs; "bowed under the burden of the wicked white man. What can we do to lighten the load of these poor children of Nature? There they lie, peacefully asleep, with their bellies full of rice. They won't awake until it is time to light the galley fire at sunset. Then they will enjoy another gorge, and turn in to forget their woes in sleep. Will they worry if the Swanee strikes a reef and sinks? No. They can swim to land. Would their master worry? Yes. He cannot swim a stroke, and, if his ship sinks, he may as well go down with it, for it represents every 'bob' he owns in the world. But these poor slaves have nothing to lose. What can we give them?"

"A stick of tobacco," said I, with a laugh; "they wouldn't give a 'thank you' for anything else. Don't saddle them with responsibilities, Cocky; just continue to carry the white man's burden."

"Pirate" Cochrane sighed again; but, like our Aboriginal seamen, I was too comfortably lazy even to talk. Out over the bows was the grey line of the Territory coast west of Darwin, the mangroves slowly taking form in darker green, a small forest-range hazily inland.

The *Swanee* was loaded with tucker and rifles and ammunition, for we were on a crocodile-shooting expedition, the skins of the big estuarine crocodile being then worth a pound apiece.

Next day we anchored in the mouth of the Finniss River. The Wangites' country this. Now, alas! the big tribes are broken up into small bands of wanderers, the once-close tribal distinctions rapidly disintegrating. I doubt if the native population along these shores is anything like the number it is supposed to be. But they are still a virile crowd, and the fairly plentiful crop of piccaninnies shows that the tribes have not yet reached that stage which is past the beginning of the end.

A few miles west was Point Blaze, where Moodoorish had killed young Renouf when his and Jim Nichol's launch was wrecked near by. As bold as brass Moodoorish's tribesmen came off in canoes to greet us - fearless types of savagery, muscular chaps, armed with shovel-bladed spears. As they stood in their canoes alongside, their eyes took in everything on deck. Several tried to climb aboard, seeking to peer below. There were lowering brows and angry mutters when we discouraged their attempted visits. It was merely for precaution's sake, however, for, in the tangled swamps and noisome creeks of that coast, "gator"-shooting can be a bit too thrilling should the hunter suddenly get the uneasy feeling that he is being stalked himself.

SOME days later a disreputable-looking little cutter came chugging in at the mouth of the river. We listened. It seemed sacrilege in that cool silence, the "phut! phut! phut!" of a spluttery little engine where the hoarse croak of a crane seemed the one fitting sound.

"Old Mitchemore," exclaimed the Pirate, "in the *Pumpkin*."

What a name! And what a craft!

The tip of her tiny mast, then her bows, then the dirty all of her appeared around the mangroves, and with furled sails she was in full view

Gathering stores for the *Pumpkin*.

The *Swanee* sailed up the river, anchoring here, anchoring there.

coming up the placid stream. She was crowded with coloured humanity, all staring towards the *Swanee*. The chug-chug of the wee engine suddenly sounded quite companionly on that lonely stream. How the little *Pumpkin* could safely sail the sea is a mystery. No doubt there is a Providence looking after sea-roamers such as these. Behind her she towed two large canoes and one so small as to appear almost a toy. A big old white man on deck waved a hairy arm, and his bull voice shouted a surprised greeting. The engine gasped, sighed, quietened. Down rattled the anchor with metallic echoes to shore, while ripples circled rapidly out. Slowly the *Pumpkin* came to rest within a stone's throw of the Swanee, bringing her smell with her, for she was packed with hundreds of salted alligator-skins. And they hum somewhat.

Old Mitchemore is a typical coastal wanderer, a nomad, forcing sea and coast to grant him a living in the wild places. His lieutenant and crack shooter was Willie, a half-caste Chinee, slim and wiry and with the alert look peculiar to the half-caste Chinee when, under the white man's guidance, he works in the farthest bush. There were several other half-caste shooters aboard, and eight daring and experienced aboriginal spearmen. Besides these, there were also a few experienced skinners, some with their families. The little old *Pumpkin* carried a packed cargo.

The old man steered this motley crowd of trained hunters from camp to camp lest harm should befall them if they were to walk through hostile country overland. Otherwise they would have been fearful of venturing across " taboo" areas. A young half-caste Japanese girl stared at us from the *Pumpkin,* and the Pirate shouted to Mitchemore to bring her aboard. He did so with alacrity. We could imagine his mouth watering at the prospect of a civilized meal aboard the well-set-up *Swanee.*

After they had climbed aboard, the girl sat with her big brown eyes set in a stare of quiet curiosity. The Pirate treated her to biscuits and jam, which she ate as a starved child would eat lollies. Old Mitchemore lived very roughly, mostly on crocodile-meat and flour. In between his own hearty mastication and his short, slow sentences, he was covertly watching Wagis, enjoying her pleasure more even than he was enjoying his own meal. He was very fond of young Wagis. She was about fifteen years old, a well-built girl, untamed as the bush she loved. While she was a tiny baby, her parents were about to strangle her, when Mitchemore luckily happened along. He "bought" the trembling infant and reared her himself. Since then she has been undisputed princess of the old man's kingdom, the mistress of any faint attempt at a plantation he might make, the real captain of the *Pumpkin*. But, when wandering in wild country, he never allowed her to venture from sight. Two of his most alert shooters formed her bodyguard. The tiny canoe astern of the *Pumpkin* was made for her, and in this we often saw her paddling about the coastal streams, quiet as the water-way itself at times, at others singing to the wilderness.

Crocodile, or "'gator," shooting is by no means easy. In fact, it requires the utmost patience, skill, and caution. No other shooting in Australasia can compare with it for thrill, nor do you feel conscience-stricken, at hitting the brutes. Then, again, there is the chance that a man shooting alone in those water-logged swamps will possibly become a victim to his prey. Among the gloomy creeks, with their muddy death-traps, the hunter, crawling about among tangled vines and rotted vegetation, must not relax his vigilance for an instant, lest he tread upon what he seeks to shoot. It is much more sporting to shoot something which, under favourable circumstances, can hit back.

But a description of crocodile-shooting either for sport or for a living would mean space. Whether or not there is a living in it at present I don't know. Skins were a good price eighteen months ago, but whether a consistent market has been captured is problematical. Suffice it to say that Mitchemore's little crowd, armed with heavy rifles; long, strong spears; and stout poles with shark hooks lashed to the end, would canoe away from the *Pumpkin*, their singing voices fading up the reaches of the river. They would seek some quiet estuary, some dark, mangrove-locked creek, or gloomy tea-tree swamp. In that noisome silence they would then hunt with the tense eagerness that primitive man has felt throughout the ages. And, for some reason, crocodile-shooting in earnest up there whisks even a "modern" man back into the realm of primitive emotions. It may be the slimy mud of the creek-banks, the mazes of the mangrove-roots, the gloom and silence, the odour of decayed vegetation, the "plop!" of things that belong to mud and shallow water. It may be the hideous, crawling, loathsome "lizards" that the hunter is seeking. I don't know. But the feeling comes into a man.

As Mitchemore hunted, we hunted, too, cruising ever along the coast as the cunning "gators" abandoned their threatened lairs. The "gator" is supposed to be brainless, whereas he possesses primitive cunning of a high order. There are various things about him which are quite contrary to one's preconceived notions. Just give his favoured creek a couple of days' hunting with rifle and spear, and he departs for pastures new. Set a trap for him and fail, and you will be lucky indeed if you get him near that same trap again.

Often we would trail the tidal creeks to where they petered out on the plain country inland. Big plains these, black soil, but not the same black soil that enriches our southern lands! The plains, covered thickly with a coarse grass, stretched far away back to dim ranges of hills. From these, at intervals, a "river" would come trickling towards the coast, to spill out in a big swamp before it reached the sea. Occasionally we would get a shot at a wandering buffalo on the plains. There are but few here, however, for the slate-grey herds roam the country away to the east, upon the Mary and Alligator Rivers. Wild pigs helped the meat larder, though; and, whenever we struck a mob of these, it meant frantic delight to the savage tribesmen. With the grass-fire roaring and with billowing smoke blinding the pigs, they would charge in all directions to the crack of rifles, the "zip" of the spear, the exultant yells of leaping huntsmen plunging amongst the smoke and flames, and maddened by the lust to kill.

There was a fair number of natives along the coast, in wandering bands here and there and in temporary camps strategically set in tangles of vine-scrub close by arms of the sea. Into those mangroves they could dive at a moment's warning, while the tidal waters brought them fish and crabs and shell-fish in plenty. Sturdy tribesmen these and independent, many of them armed with that terrible and highly-prized possession the shovel-bladed spear. Their pleasant struggle for existence keeps them very much alive-the men, the wild-eyed women, and the pot-bellied imps of youngsters. They need to be alert, for ceaseless vendettas are going on amongst them. Vengeance parties, consisting of bands of half a dozen sombre-painted, grim-faced warriors, are continually travelling the land. Imagine the hushed excitement, the fearful glances, when news comes that one of these killer bands is in the locality! The whole camp will often disappear more speedily than ever Arab folded his tent and vanished away.

Not that they are not game, for among these very men were they who had attacked Mounted Constable Hemmings and Hoffman's patrol, and wounded several trackers. These chaps have sought more than one brush with the Mounted Police, yet they flee from the vengeance bands. The law of an eye for an eye knows not mercy.

As we gradually worked along the coast, life dreamed by with unceasing interest. We were continually seeking and not always finding safe anchorage, continually paddling up new creeks, each one of which had its half-dozen "old man" "gators" and its host of twelve-footers. We knew the pleasant thrill of stealthily ascending a jungle-locked creek for the first time, and of peering around every bend for the first sight of some basking monster. Then the continual trips inland, the new swamps and lagoons, plains and ranges, the new natives we met! It is easy to understand why some men like the life. One morning we sailed into the mouth of the Daly River. A fine, broad waterway this, navigable for small craft for some sixty miles upstream, where one finds a police station and a little peanut settlement. The broad, muddy water, lashed by furious tides, meanders through plains from the bamboo thickets far upstream. Down the river there is no settlement. Westward from here past the Fitzmaurice and on to the rugged Victoria, it is all wild natives' country, Nemarluk's country in particular. It was throughout this pathless tangle that the Big Chief defied the police so long. There have been some epic chases across that country after Nemarluk's "Red Band" and "Tiger's Mob" in particular, though other bands also have taken violent action against the lone white man. A little west is Treachery Bay, where Nemarluk's "Red Band" killed Nagata, the Japanese captain of the lugger Ouida, then boarded the vessel and killed Yoshida and Owashi. There was a wild and woolly chase then after the crew, who had fled for their lives in the dinghy. But Nemarluk's inexperienced sailormen ran the *Ouida* up on a sandbank, and the pursuers had to be content with sacking her. Thus started Nemarluk on his exciting career.

A little farther west is the tangled maze of the Fitzmaurice. It was here that "Tiger's Mob" cruelly murdered Stephens and Cook. A much less likeable type of the virile primitive is Tiger, a low-browed killer. It is seldom that white men venture into that country. Occasionally a couple of lonely prospectors intrude, or a dingo-shooter hoping for a big haul in untried country - just these, and the patrols of the Mounted Police.

The area along the coast is thickly mangrove-fringed and intersected by numerous arms of the sea and by tidal creeks hedged with vine-scrub alternating with grassy forest. Farther inland are big plains, which run on into sloping country, bush-covered and stretching away to a series of rocky ranges. Away over those ranges is some of the big cattle-country, while away west is the Victoria River, perhaps the most picturesque stream in the Territory.

ONE morning, while the *Swanee* lay at anchor, a wild yell caused our seamen to glance apprehensively shoreward. A naked warrior stood there. Again his wild cry, echoed far up the river. In a few minutes fifty painted tribesmen were staring from the banks, the dark heads of timid ones peering like shaggy black crows from the low tree-branches.

All of them were naked, all were ochred with white and red bars across chest and limbs and forehead. Some wore the human hair belt of the warrior, numbers wore a headband tufted with cockatoo feathers. We stared curiously, for the wild man is always an interesting sight. But these in certain respects were a disappointment. Four of them could speak a little guttural "pidgin," while all except ten had seen white men before. There are very few places remaining in Australia to-day where the natives have not seen a white man. These tribesmen were a travelling band from the Fitzmaurice. It is by such wanderings that the last of the wild Territory tribes is fast becoming "civilized." Tribal boundaries are already broken. Bands of men travel now east to make contact with the settlement at the Daly; some travel still farther east, towards Darwin. The white man possesses some irresistible attraction to the black, and once the native and his people make contact with an isolated settlement the tribe is doomed. It is a pity. I should like to see Arnhem Land and this other last wild area west of the Daly left entirely to the primitive peoples. But they themselves are increasingly seeking the whites.

In a heavy wet season in this area, big rivers spill out over the low country and turn it in places into a marshy sea. The natives then cling to the coastline or retire inland to the ranges, whose wild gorges and cave-systems make ideal wet-weather camps. When the wet season ends and the excess waters drain gradually away, the nomads come down to the plains, already a sea of green, under grass that in some areas is growing five feet high. Plentiful lagoons gleam far and wide over the land; great hosts of wildfowl circle the swamps and breed in countless thousands in morass and lagoon. Especially is this so in the Moil country, which is a paradise of wild life to the native huntsman. The last of the rain-clouds drifts away, the sun shines with undimmed brilliance, the earth is warm, the air is sweet; everything is growing, bursting with life. The Aboriginal and his wife and youngsters gorge themselves to repletion, then turn their attention to the new seasonal corroborees, held on age-old meeting-grounds of the tribes. After these festivals the earth is filled with new life again, and all things must get ready to battle through the dry season. The tribes split up into sub-tribes, into hordes, into wandering bands, and the old nomadic life is in full swing again. Tribal quarrels, vendettas, sorcery, hunting, all take their normal trend as Destiny has ordained.

The *Swanee* sailed up the river, anchoring here, anchoring there, while we in the dinghies stealthily paddled ahead, firing again and again at the long grey shapes sunning themselves on the mud-banks. At last a day came when the first report of a rifle would send every "gator" miles away slithering to the water. So we faced the open sea, then headed along the coast again, seeking some inlet undisturbed by sound of gun.

And, no matter where we went, there arose the signal-smokes of the wild man, telling his mates the white man had come.

# 8

# Pearls

HEEDLESS of the throb of the big war-drums, the boom of the Boo, the roar of warriors' voices, Captain Banner sat quietly unperturbed. A black-bearded giant this man, a wanderer from the South Seas! His brig, the Julia Percy, lay anchored by the Warrior Reefs, every man standing to arms. Alongside Banner squatted Kebisu, the Mamoose of Tutu, a giant with enormous shoulder-muscles, the greatest fighting chief the Coral Sea had ever known. Flaring torches illumined these organized warriors, now stamping into the war-dance fury, the faces of women vivid amongst the blackness of the palms. Soon their dance would come with screaming song to fan the warrior blood-lust, while the screech of their Goa-nut rattles, the sway of glistening bodies, would fan all into hysteria. Kebisu remained motionless, frowning, his Gaba-gaba war club thonged to a powerful wrist. Banner watched interestedly, friendly and unsuspicious of face.

But a whaleboat crowded with armed men was drifting inshore, ready instantly, if necessary, to back him up.

In all his battling life Banner never desired peace so ardently as he did now. For lying among the cooking fires were hundreds of pearl-shells, each actually as large as a plate, while thousands lay thrown upon the sands and beaches. Beautiful mother-of-pearl, carelessly thrown on the fires until the agonized oyster within popped open its shell to stew in its own juice.

Such big shell Banner had only dreamed of before. Among

those great coral reefs beyond the shadows of the palms must lie the richest pearl-shell bed in the world.

As indeed it proved to be.

But what made Banner's eyes stick out like walnuts was the sight of a great pearl thrown from greasy fingers to the sands.

Roasted pearls! thrown among the sands!

Of what use were pearls to these people? True, a few wore them in their ears and one big brown warrior sported a bunch of them like liquid grapes dangling from his nose.

No. Above all things Banner desired not only peace but a friendly alliance.

He came to terms with Kebisu.

Both were remarkable men. One saw limitless fortune almost within his grasp; the other sat glowering under the strangest premonition of the end of all things for his people. It was this indecision that swayed the balance. A curious, almost armed friendship developed between these two men, a friendship that lasted until the death of Banner.

Thus were found the rich pearl-shell beds of the Coral Sea. Soon, there started the great pearl-shell rushes, more romantic, more exciting than any gold-rush. From the little capitals of Melbourne and Sydney far away to the south the tiny vessels sailed up along the north-east Queensland coast under every stitch of canvas their creaking yards could carry, schooners and brigantines, barques and ketches and luggers. The next fifty years brought a wealth of romance and adventure that would pale into insignificance the most colourful stories of romantic fiction. Here, tiny vessels voyaged two thousand miles and more to enter an uncharted sea that was and is a maze of the most intricate reefs in the world.

They sailed along the 1,200 miles of the Great Barrier Reef and into the Coral Sea with its thousands of square miles of beautiful but treacherous inner reefs, its sandbanks and uncharted channels that became

Top: A pearling lugger, the *Chrisrina*, in the Torres Strait.
Below: Pearling luggersin the harbour at Broome, 1917.

the boneyards of the Dons and the earliest Dutch. Here are eight months of calm blue seas, warmly sunlit, followed swiftly by leaden skies and fury of white squall and black, by shrieking, howling, roaring cyclones. How the fleets up-anchored and sailed away before each cyclone season came! From sheltering island far and wide like fearful birds, they flew south to the safety of calmer seas, to riotous nights in Brisbane, Sydney, and Melbourne.

Loaded with pearl shell, drunk with pearls.

And the next season they would come sailing back with numbers increased by tales of pearls and lagoons and brown-skinned maids laughing under the palms.

But many a vessel never returned. Coral ripped the bottoms from some; others were attacked by canoe-loads of befeathered warriors and the crews were clubbed to a man. Others met mutiny with blood fights among the crew. Many an islet in the Coral Sea has its now almost forgotten tale of marooning. Some such stories are sad, others are very cruel. Then there is high romance in various individuals who elected to cast adrift from their fellows and form an island kingdom all their own. Most of these would-be sultans were clubbed when they landed to take possession of their kingdoms, but several, of rare initiative and utter fearlessness, succeeded and found their heart's desire. Ruling with a strong but understanding hand, they survived, and, in at least one particular instance that I know of well, the white "king" fitted the islanders to survive against the whites and was a deeply-mourned man when at last he went on his last voyage to Boigu, Isle of the Blest. His memory is still green, his son now rules in his place. This man is not Baba, Father of Mer, whose recent death is deeply mourned.

Both men were of entirely different types, but both loved the islanders and each spent his life in training them to survive against the whites.

With years, came organization. The freelance vessels began to combine together as fleets. The richness of the pearl-shell beds brought plentiful money, and much of this was spent in the building of larger vessels. It is surprising the number of vessels that were built in Australia in those days.

In course of time Jardine came to Somerset to form another "Singapore." On the wee cliffs facing Albany Pass, the "great house" and "barracks" were built. The "Parade Ground" echoed to martial tread. Guns frowned down over the turbulent Pass. "Streets" were "laid out" in readiness for the coming city. In military style, the flag came down at sunset.

Jardine's story is a great romance. But his dream-city has long since gone back to wild bush, while Jardine, side by side with his Samoan princess wife, sleeps down below in the tiny beach.

Soon after the fiery Chester took possession of Thursday Island as Government Resident, the island became a definite white base for the pearling fleets. The memory of noted vessels both of good and of notorious repute is still green among the old hands up there. For years afterwards fighting occurred ever and anon between the crews of wandering pearling vessels and the fierce warriors of the numerous islands. But "civilization" was coming. Disease spread amongst the islanders, complete island populations were wiped out, the fine warriors of Tutu amongst them. Thus Kebisu's premonition came true.

Fortunately, not all the islands shared the same fate. What remains of the Torres Strait islanders is the virile population to-day.

THEN to the pearling, fleets came the days of the Hell Ships. These were large schooners, one to a fleet. They provisioned the fleets and sailed with the shell back to Thursday Island. Thus the fleets were enabled to keep the sea throughout the eight months of the fishing season.

It was a great day for a fleet when the sails of a schooner arrived.

Up came the divers from below, up came the anchors as the schooner ran up a flag. Up went the sails as all the little vessels came sailing to cluster around her. Busy work then in unloading stores and water to the smaller vessels among a babel of voices in many tongues, coarse jokes from the South Sea bo'suns as they unloaded pearl-shell up on to the schooner. The white skippers crowded aboard, eager for news, eager to show their pearls and have them weighed and deposited in the big iron safe. Then the slop-chest was opened, a huge store down below stacked with all that a sailorman loves to buy, including grog. Around a Hell Ship which dealt largely in grog, pandemonium would soon break loose. The masters and portion of the crews were hard-bitten whites, but the majority were coloured seamen from all the South Seas. Malays, Rotomah men, Filipinos, Rarotongans, Tanna men, Torres Islanders, Polynesians, New Hebrides men, Kanakas, men from all the islands, with a sprinkling of Chinese. Hell broke loose amongst them while the white masters were arguing over pearls in the schooner's cabin. When the schooner sailed away, she left Hell behind her in the fleet until the grog was all done.

During the first years of the pearl-shell rushes the shell was easily found and collected among the reefs at low water. As the years passed, the shell had to be located and dived for in ever-deepening water. White men dived, but soon found that the South Sea men and Torres Strait Islanders were infinitely better divers than they. As the easily-worked shell in shallow waters became worked out, diving dresses were imported from England. White men filled these dresses for a while; but, as every man's ambition was to become a master pearler and own a vessel of his own, it was not long before they had trained Malays and Manilamen and Rotomah men in particular, and a sprinkling of Chinese to the diving dress. After the era of the Hell Ships the Japanese began to make their appearance. These quiet, painstaking, quick-learning, thoroughly efficient and fatalistic men presently began to make their mark. They gave no trouble, no work was too hard, no day too long, no risk too great. They began to plant their graveyards. What did they care? Nothing. If a man has to die, he has to die, and there are plenty more men in the world. Gradually they learned the game, they stuck to it, their numbers steadily increased, their hold strengthened imperceptibly throughout all the fleets.

Meanwhile, the white skippers of all the fleets were constantly seeking new shell-beds. They built Thursday Island into a town and an important port, they sailed the entire length of the Great Barrier Reef, sailed all the Coral Sea and up along the coasts of New Guinea, tried the Cape York Peninsula coast, and sailed round into the Gulf and Arafura. They did marvellous work, quite unsung, in the tiniest of craft. They developed the *beche-de-mer* industry. Millions of pounds in shell and pearls was won around 6,000 miles of our coasts to swell the wealth and prosperity of Australia.

On the western side of the continent a certain William Tays on the beach at Nickol Bay had picked up pearl-shell away back in 1861. Thus started pearling in the West. At first, shell was picked up by hand along the reefs at low tide. Aborigines were increasingly employed. They gathered in the course of years hundreds of thousands of pounds' worth' of shell for flour and rice and trade tobacco. Small vessels appeared, the forerunner of fleets. The Shark's Bay pearling-grounds were found. Gradually the little free-lance vessels crept farther north up that inhospitable, uninhabited coast. The western rush set in in earnest. Then "rushes" of free-lance vessels sailed still farther north, forming a base here and there that was to be the nucleus of a future township. Wild and woolly were the "camps" occasionally, for in great degree men were a law unto themselves. Huge camps they necessarily were, because for over 1,000 miles this coastline was uninhabited, and big bases had to be formed for stores. The pearling-fleets actually developed much of our northern coastline.

At last the fleets had ventured far north. They crept into Roebuck Bay, where the great old buccaneer-navigator Dampier had sailed the little

Top: Pearling luggars off Thursday Island in the early 1920s.
Bottom: Japanese pearling crew off Broome about 1932.

*Roebuck* in 1699. The natives still say that his ghost can be seen on moonlit nights gazing out to sea from Buccaneer Rock. Roebuck Bay was sheltered; it was in the heart of rich pearling-grounds, and here the sea-wanderers eventually formed their main camp of Broome. This was destined to grow into the richest pearl and pearl-shell town in the world, to become the base and home of men who feared little and dared greatly, and was to be blessed by rich prosperity for fifty years. From this base, ever-increasing fleets sailed north and south, finding vast shell beds, rich occasionally in pearl. A township soon sprang up, colourful in life and endeavour. Fortunes were won in shell and pearls.

The loveliest gems of the sea came from Broome waters. Kings and emperors were to buy them, millionaires all over the world and Indian rajahs were to bid for them. The pearlers who won them (alas, often at dreadful cost) were to receive hardly one-tenth of their sales-value. Fortunes were made, too, in pearl-buying. Buyers came from all over the world, but the greatest buyers of all were Australians, gifted men "born to pearls." Several came there who had not seen a pearl in their lives except in jewellers' windows. They lived to sell their gems in London, Vienna, Paris, India, New York, and Berlin.

But, though Fortune brought the mantle of Pearl King to some, she proved a deceitful jade to others. Some pearlers struggled all their lives and just made a do of it. Theirs was never the luck to find rich pearls or prolific shell-beds; or, if they did so, the market tumbled down at a critical time. Pearling has always been for the shell; it is the shell that pays. If a good pearl is found now and then, well-that is the great good luck of the finder. Other men started with nothing, then managed to secure a share in a lugger. The first voyage of such a shareholder might prove highly successful. Delighted, he then would buy a lugger of his own. In a very few years he probably would own a fleet. And a Willy Willy would sink his fleet in a night. Or a period of bad luck in other forms would bring him right down to where he had started. Such is the luck of the game.

And the life is hard. Months at sea, alone with coloured seamen, and cockroaches, and the smell of fish and Asiatic foods, and the constant roll, roll, roll of the Indian Ocean.

Coloured men of almost every nationality crowded Broome at times. The town was the "White Town," "Yokohama," and "Chinatown," otherwise the European quarter and the Asiatic town. The white pearlers built their pretty bungalows and business-like stores, while the others crowded into "Asiatic Town." That place was seething for years under all manner of fortune and intrigue, the covert selling of stolen pearls, the whisperings of "snide" buyers, the schemes of the coloured "heads," all manner of conspiracies.

As the years went by, the fleets crept ever farther north until their bows turned east around the north-west corner into the Timar. That corner to-day is still the wildest portion of the Australian coastline-hundreds of miles of frowning cliffs, of giant fiords out of which come roaring tide-rips, creating an inferno of whirlpools. Just like the pearling fleets 3,000 miles cast on the north-eastern coastline, the fleets here feared their Willy Willy season, a sea-devil revolving in a roaring black cloud wreaking destruction on sea and land. But, for eight months of the year, the weather, though often hot, is beautiful, the Indian Ocean moderately calm-in spots. The north-western pearlers had no Great Barrier Reef nor Coral Sea with its lagoons and palm-girt islands and fighting Islanders of a fairly cultured race. Instead, they had the great Eighty Mile Beach, which has been the grave of fleets of vessels and hundreds of men. Farther north they had the rugged coast with Archipelagoes inhabited sparsely by aborigines, the wild mainland thickly. Tragedies occurred there when crews of wrecked vessels were massacred.

Pearling for the start on the north-western coast was done by "hand-shelling," combing the reefs at low tide. Then by tiny vessels manned by white and aboriginal divers. Then native and coloured "skin" divers were introduced. Then the diving dress manned by white divers. As on the north-eastern coast, it was soon found that Malays and Rotomah men could "learn the diving-dress" efficiently. There came the era of the fleets and the "mother-ships." Then, as on the north-eastern coast, the Japanese began to drift in.

With several thousand or more coloured seamen among all the fleets, it was inevitable that trouble should occasionally occur, either on shore or afloat. These men were of different races, often of antagonistic religions. In various instances they nursed grudges of centuries, while their present life was a hotbed of intrigue and jealousy. This factor helped the few white men to master them. For, although one faction might wish to loaf or thieve the pearls or murder the skipper and make away with the ship, the rival faction would betray them to the skipper. So, for many years, practically all fleets took to sea with each vessel manned by mixed crews. Japanese and Koepangers, or Malays and Manilamen, South Sea men and aborigines and Amboinese. Even so, there have been some fiery clashes, especially during the cyclone season, which is lay-up season ashore. Bitter resentment, racial jealousies, smouldering hatreds have burst out as hundreds of coloured men came roaring through the town brandishing clubs and knives. Both Broome and Thursday Island have experienced these dreaded racial riots when the coloured seamen went raving mad. But such occurrences are rare, as is mutiny at sea. Mutiny and apparent mutiny actually have occurred, followed by the total disappearance of a vessel. Perhaps the mutineers had been wrecked, or more likely, had sought safety in the Dutch East Indies or the Philippines. One such band mutinied while almost within sight of Broome, killed the captain and mate and the captain's son, and later knifed several of the crew, who had indiscreetly showed they remained loyal. They had just heaved the bodies overboard when a schooner came along to "talk." The mutineers stood away, and rushed the arms on deck. The schooner then stood away, wondering at the manoeuvres of the other vessel. The mutineers cleared for Koepang, sank the schooner when near there, and rowed ashore.

They explained to the Dutch authorities that they had been wrecked and had taken to the whaleboats. But John Chi the cook put them away. They were arrested and returned to Australia, where the ringleaders swung in Fremantle gaol. Several of these men proved to be notorious in insurrection in the Philippines.

But the War year came. Gone were the roaring days; modernity and depression had come instead. The bottom dropped out of the pearl and pearl-shell market. It has only just begun to recover during these last two years.

By War time, a great change had come over both the working and the personnel of the fleets along both the north-eastern and the north-western coasts. The white men were still masters, but those along the north-eastern coast took their vessels to sea no more. All the divers, tenders, and most of the crews were now organized Japanese. They practically made their own terms with the masters. And by now one of those terms was that they be allowed to keep- all the pearls won!

On the north-western coast, Australian skippers with white shell-openers still took their vessels to sea, as they do to-day, but fewer and fewer whites go to sea. The divers and tenders were mainly Japanese and a few Malays, the crews were Japanese and Malays, Koepangers, and a few Manilamen.

The Japanese had their powerfully-organized Japanese Club and fought for advantage after advantage against the Aus-tralian owners. For years after the War the industry languished. Several pearlers established themselves in Darwin, prospecting the Arafura in the hope of finding rich shell-beds in that great area of sea. Eventually they did so, extraordinarily rich shell-beds were located there but a very few years ago.

By now, the pearling vessels had evolved a type of swift and seaworthy lugger, those built on the north-eastern seaboard being particularly graceful. And now, engines were installed, air-compressors installed, too, in place of the old-type hand air-pump. The divers and tenders were highly-trained men, making good money; they were indentured from Japan. Each man required four years to train, but even then he might prove a bad investment, for it is only a percentage among them that become first-class divers.

The finding of the great pearl shell beds in the Arafura came in the nick of time. The shell at first was very easily won, which compensated for its low price.

The master pearlers for years now on each coast had experienced a struggle to fit their vessels for sea each season. After the discovery of the rich beds in the Arafura, fleets were quickly formed at Darwin. It is now an important pearling centre.

And now a cloud came upon the horizon, the writing on the wall that points to world events. An occasional strange lugger was sighted, fishing in the northern seas - a well-equipped lugger manned by Japanese, with divers who had been trained by years of work in the Australian fleets. Little notice was taken, until in three years' time a fleet of Japanese vessels was fishing off the coast. And some of these vessels were larger, more modern than the Australian. Where a modernly-equipped Australian lugger could send down two divers, a similar Japanese vessel could send down three.

Last year, the fleet was almost equal in size to the Australian fleets, and fished apparently as much shell. Next year?

Very luckily, the appearance of the Japanese fleet corresponded with the rise in shell, England and America buying and consuming huge quantities.

If only the world continues to ask for and consumes more and more shell, all will be well. If not?

Such is an outline of the history of our pearling industry to the present day. The master pearlers and the scene of their operations are far away, but we should bear these men and their activities well in mind. It is the pearlers who opened up 6,000 miles of our northern coastline, who are mainly responsible for planting the few townships that we have there. But for them, the far north to-day might boast of only three tiny cattle-ports.

Just think of it!

# 9

# Romance of the Coral Seas

BLUE is the sea around Prince of Wales Island, all shadowed the waterway from the scrubby hills of Hammond. The tiny port of Thursday Island is pretty with its white houses and bright under sunlight glinting on the wings of the pearling fleet as vessel after vessel slips away. We sail in our lugger in good company out past the palms of Horn Island, and we come to sea with a lazy breeze and adventure before us. Whither shall we go? Roughly nor'-east? There it shall be, and we'll cross the ghostly tracks of mighty sea rovers who have gone before. Torres, that man with the heart of a lion braving unknown perils of land and sea in his tiny vessel. One glance astern. There lies Possession Island, where Cook planted the flag. And Murralug, scene of disasters to ships, men, and women. Here the frigate *Blanche* chased her blackbirders, here sailed Jardine when he was autocrat of the Strait while that scallywag of the seas, Nicholas the Greek, slipped by. And now our bow points towards the waters of Bligh, chased from Warrior Island by the fiercest fighters of the Strait. Should wind and time permit, we'll visit that tiny isle, made a little Britain of by Kebisu, greatest chief of the Strait. And now east, far out there on the Great Barrier, is where the *Pandora* went down in a smother of foam, grinding coral, shrieking timbers. Spanish dons, Portuguese captains, lion-hearted Dutchmen sailed these treacherous waters before those old English sea dogs came nosing along. Many a forgotten craft lies deep below, their old ribs now solid coral. We keep a sharp lookout lest we, too, strike the jagged teeth and go down to oblivion to sink choking within the lovely sea gardens below. Our coloured seamen swear that sea-maids do really lurk there below, gazing up and waiting for surface-men to come gasping down to their arms.

We pass the Peak of Naghir as it rises sheer out of the sea, and the crew boys laugh uproariously, for here lived until his sins claimed him a cunning old South Sea islander, bos'n in the days of the hell-ships. A huge stone jutting from the Peak of Naghir is supposed by the natives to be the god of the island turned into living stone. A precipitous track lies before the god. Passing villagers always walked quickly there with bowed heads, not daring to look up. And one day young Samsu, he of the broad chest and great muscles that could speed him diving deep below, stood suddenly in terror. For a deep, sepulchral voice came from the god.

"Samsu! During one full moon you must dive for pearl-shell. And willingly you must give all to my good brother, the South Sea islander. And expect nothing in payment, for you shall receive none. Begone! And dive deep and truly for my brother, lest something very terrible befall you."

Thus, for years, did the cunning old South Sea man work upon the superstitions of the islanders to his exceeding profit and content.

The day dreams by under a beautiful blue sky, and with waves so lazy they can hardly rise to the bows. If you listen hard, you can hear the lugger swinging, the little sighings and creakings of cordage and timber that tell of a good tight ship.

And there! Starboard! A cloud of darting foam and now a thunder-clap! Strange, there's not a cloud in the sky! Another thunder-clap, an exclamation from the boys standing in the bows! All is explained. It is a school of Devil-bats harrying an enormous shoal of fish. The ocean for a quarter-mile long, three hundred yards wide, is a seething mass of foam from packed fish. Millions and millions of them! Heavens! Where is our Australian and British capital and enterprise that they have not already erected canneries on these islands, that our own Australian-manned trawling-fleets are not reaping the harvest of this wonderful Coral Sea!

MAINO, SON OF THE GREAT KEBISU, LAST MAMOOSE
OF TUTU AND YAM

(Holding his father's famous *gaba-gaba*.)

As the great shoal speeds by, we gaze astonished at the cloud of foam and flashing silver. Soon, though, will a huge black blanket rise from the sea and fall back with booming clap of mighty "wings." So the great Sea-bats thunder their prey together, then rush among them like torpedoes.

What delight for the tourists of the world, out here in this blue sea with its palm-clad islands, its historic romance, its mighty fish!

We pass the Two Brothers islands. Strangely quiet they look, abandoned, their foreshores thickly cluttered with queer black stones. The crew boys are whispering. Those stones, they say, are the bodies of slain people, massacred in a raid by the great chief Kebisu.

From his head-quarters at Warrior Island he sailed, his twenty-eight huge war canoes packed with men. The men on the Two Brothers had refused tribute to Kebisu, great Mamoose, who claimed tribute from all between the Great South Land and the barbarous country of New Guinea.

In the dead of night Kebisu landed, and the villagers awoke in hell. Burning arrows flaming into their thatched houses, painted men in waving head-dress hacking and clubbing and yelling to the shriek of the rattles and thrumming of the doad. Only one terrible howl: "Kill!" "Kill!" "Kill!"

They massacred every soul on the Two Brothers.

Just for cussedness sake we'll slew off the course and head for Moa Island. We've a month's cruising ahead and can't possibly visit all the islands by then. So we'll simply poke about and land on any we fancy on the spur of the moment.

Moa rises like a big cloud that develops into the mountain of Moa. It's not a big mountain at all, but it looks a monster as its scrub-clad mass rises from the sea. There are very many stories of Moa, both of the island and of the mountain; but one that always haunted me was that of the frightened Lamar with the golden hair. A Lamar, to the Torres Strait

Luckily the terrible urge that drives these rats ever on caused the plague to islanders, was a living spirit returned to earth. If allowed to step on land and live, such a spirit could wreak untold harm. Which explains why so many castaways in years gone by were immediately clubbed when they stepped ashore. Any white person to these people was a Lamar, a living spirit from another world. A boat-load of castaways landed on Moa; among them a young woman with long hair that hung almost to her knees. The islanders described it as a cloak of hair that had been kissed yellow-red by the sun. The warriors clubbed the men, and during those fierce moments, the girl fled, screaming. There was nowhere for her to fly to but the gloomy mountain of Moa. The islanders laughed as they finished their work, she would be good sport later, hunting her up there amongst that undergrowth.

But they never found her.

They combed and combed the mountain. She had vanished. Puzzled, they searched every yard of the island. It is a big island, all little hills and valleys, but the islanders knew every foot of it. They never found her. To this day they wonder what happened to her. Their fathers, of course, at last believed she had taken spirit form and from the summit of Moa fled to the skies.

Gazing out from that hoary old summit, I often wondered. The distracted girl could only have crawled into a cave. But every cave is known to the islanders. There is the great cave to where all the women and old people were rushed when the blackbirders came. When the sails of a woman raider were sighted, the Boo shell warned all the island, and the women rushed to the great cave.

But there are other subterranean mysteries of which the islanders even to-day dare not speak. The Sacred Cave of the Great Au-Guud, down into which none dared enter save the Zogo-le. And only to them was its secret entrance known. What if by the millionth chance the clawing hands of the terrified girl had stumbled upon that entrance? More likely some cunning Maid-le sorcerer had watched her, then beckoned her. She would have followed anything that seemed to promise the remotest chance of safety.

Somehow, I always hoped the girl had not found the way down to the bowels of the earth, to the nethermost kingdoms of the Great Auguud, to the huge carved masks of the Zogo-le, to the Sacred Skulls glaring from their painted ledges deep below.

WE'LL anchor a while at Moa and enjoy a prowl round. Here's a surprise. The tiny village of St. Paul's, and a little coral church, prettily white under the hills. Missionary Schomberg has recently done this job, and died in the doing of it. In trutl a labour of love! Gone now is the Zogo House and the big black Zogo stone once anointed with human oil. Gone, too, are the huge white sacrificial shells that held the blood of human sacrifices. The entrance to the great Zogo cave has been stoned up by the last of the Zogo-le; undergrowth and young trees have been planted upon it. Few indeed of the inhabitants know where the entrance was; not one dare tell. He would disappear - for ever.

We walk over the hills and down the pleasant dales of Moa. Brilliant sunlight, hum of insects, scent of flower and tree! Trilling rivulets here and there, flowering vines upon sapling and palm! Birds sing cheerily. 'Tis good to be alive. With an itchy feeling on the back, too, as we climb some rugged path down into a ravine for on these hills up in the trees there lives a small "flying goanna," a green fellow with quaint membranes under his armpits. As you pass by in open-necked shirt he is liable to spiral down from the greenery and fasten teeth and claw in your neck and back. It seldom happens, but I saw it twice. And, oh, my, what a scatter!

In a few hours' walk we are at Moa village, nestling under the palms. Before us gleams a beautiful waterway like a wide, calm river dotted with canoes, echoing voices of laughing people. Opposite is big

Badu Island, with the long village all little brown houses under those avenues of palms. Farther back, the rocky, forest-clad hills of Badu rise strangely reminiscent of the sunlit hills of Northern Australia. But who'd think we had islands like these in Australia!

What a base for a trawling-fleet, or what an idyll for tourist chateaux, these two big islands with only that calm waterway dividing them. But I set out to lead you a cruise through the Coral Sea. And here we are at Moa, anchored at the first sunset!

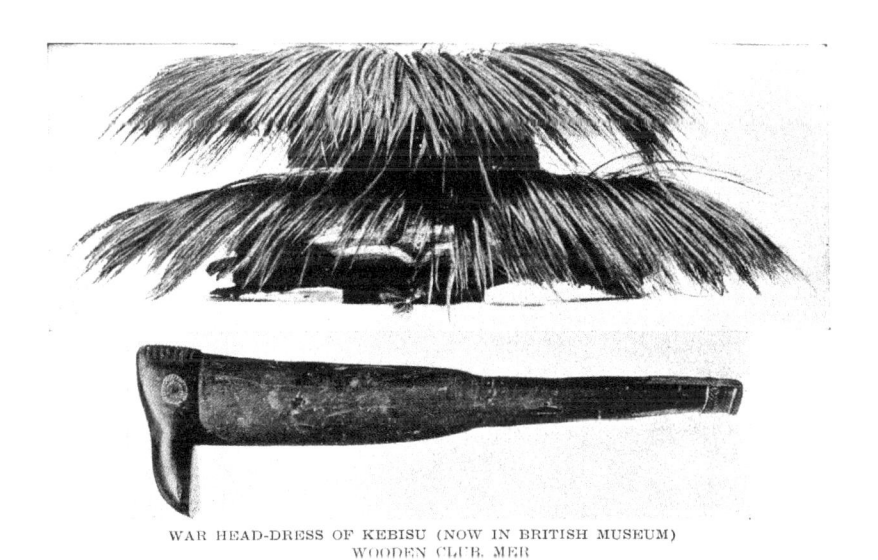

WAR HEAD-DRESS OF KEBISU (NOW IN BRITISH MUSEUM)
WOODEN CLUB, MER

# 10

# The Amazon Gins

*Quite a number of readers of the "Sydney Morning Herald" have asked me whether I ever heard of the "Amazon Gins" as described by Mr. W H Rudd, in the December 28 Issue of the "Herald."*

The article mentioned was quite correct, and brought back memories to me. As a young fellow, while prospecting in the dense jungle ranges behind the Daintree (North Queensland), I had often tried to coax our aboriginal boys to take me to the country of the "amazon gins," but without avail. The huge bulk of the gloomy mountain, its crown often cloaked in mist, loomed up across the valley from our half-way camp. Mt Alexander side by side with Mt Peter Botte, whose "Stone Sisters" are a landmark to mariners far at sea. There is an interesting legend attached to those Stone Sisters, too.

It is in the labyrinths of Mt Alexander that the tribe of Amazons are supposed to hold sway. The belief is only a legend, of course, but is believed to be fact by the present-day aboriginals. No native will go closer than three miles to the base of the mountain, let alone venture into the valleys and jungle scrubs that hedge it round. My mates at the time were two educated half-castes who also were acknowledged as the leaders and advisers of the Daintree, China Camp, and Bloomfield River tribes. They had absolute control over these 1000 natives (the two big influenza epidemics, alas, have almost wiped out these aboriginal friends of mine) but the brothers could not induce any of their hench-men to take me to the mountain and explore. Neither would the brothers come with me. To venture alone would have been a big job besides which I might easily have offended the men with whose tribe I roamed.

The Amazons are supposed to be a tribe of giant women warriors who can run faster than a man, and throw a longer spear further than a man They are a fierce, athletic tribe of furies hunting over the spurs of their big mountain in packs. Should they see tracks of a man within their boundaries they immediately raise the hue and cry, which in shrill piercing screams goes echoing up the valleys, floating from crag to crag. Then they give chase and never stop until they catch the man. They tear him to pieces, rend him limb from limb.

No wonder my aboriginal friends would not venture with me to the land of the Amazon Gins, they used to make my spine "creep" with their descriptions of how the Gins kill a man. To listen to them talking though, was impressive of their deep belief. We would be sitting down among the sweet forest grass at the jungle edge, gazing across the blue valley at the hazy bulk of Mt Alexander. Our bags of flour and cases of provisions where we had dropped them, each warrior's spears close to hand, the dogs at the forest edge scenting a tree-climbing 'roo. After a long climb up the precipitous spurs, we would be resting, preparatory to plunging into the jungle. In low tones the tribesmen would discuss the furies across the valley, telling me of their intimate life with such detail that at times I found myself vaguely wondering if there could be some shadow of fact In the belief. There is not, of course. An old man used often to travel with us. He had lost one arm, how, even my two half-caste mates could not tell me. But every aboriginal within a radius of 200 miles knew. The Amazon Gins had pulled that arm from its socket! He was the only man within their memory who had been caught by and yet escaped the Gins. His story of the happening was vivid in detail and uncannily convincing, but is rather long to tell here. However, not only all the tribes but he himself believed that his arm had been torn from his body by the Gins.

These Gins keep a few men, selected specimens of magnificent manhood, but utter slaves. They are kept necessarily for breeding purposes alone. Otherwise, they are harshly treated, the builders of the gunyahs, the wood and water carriers for the Gins They are not allowed to stray from camp, and when the Gins move camp they are loaded up like pack animals. Male babies are allowed to live long enough to be judged as to their future physical development. The pick of them are then allowed to live, the others are killed. The female babies all survive, except any weakly ones, who are knocked on the head. The gins love their female babies, but it is a crying disgrace to bear a man-child, and sometimes, in a fury, the Gin who has been so disgraced will seize a fighting stick and belabour the nearest man into insensibility. It is probable that after she has finished with him, he will not be capable of being a father any more.

From earliest childhood the girl babies are trained in tracking, spear throwing, endurance, running, and more severe athletic exercises They are trained to regard men as fiends to be run down and killed at every possible chance. The discipline of the tribe is very strict, its destiny is guided by the Council of the Women, to disobey whom means death.

The full details and history of this alleged Amazon tribe, as told me by my aboriginal friends is deeply interesting, but I think I've told enough here to assure readers that Mr Rudd's account is quite correct. One further thing I might mention though, just to assure readers that these wild she-women are not nice girls to meet. They love snakes! As the Gins move from camp to camp their tame snakes rustle through the grass after them. On sunny afternoons, lying among the gunyahs the snakes coil up at the feet of the gins. Should a sudden alarm be raised, the snakes slither down the gins' mouths, out of which their heads hiss towards the expected danger.

Occasionally, by accident, one of the men slaves will kill a snake, probably by dropping a heavy load of wood upon it. He has little time to regret the mishap, for the Gins tear him to pieces.

By many other hair-raislng stories I was solemnly warned against ever venturing into the country of the Amazon Gins. Being young and a bit romantic in those days, I used to wonder whether they would treat a white man as they would a black stranger, or would they-?

Being a small man, and not a dashing Samson, I let well alone, but would dearly have loved a roam over the big old mountain.

There may be gold there.

# 11

# Rats

ARMIES of scurrying rats, millions of them pressing feverishly onward. Over hill and plain like rippling brown clouds upon the earth, devouring everything eatable in their path. When they rustled across a bush road their countless hurrying feet brushed smooth the ruts.

Springing from and keeping to the far out lands, they battled their frantic way down one of the driest areas in Australia. The earth, burned and cracked by the sun, supported only the hardiest and scantiest of stunted vegetation. Across it all for hundreds of miles scurried the millions of tiny feet.

What instinct was it that kept them far west of the rivers country? The rivers they had to cross were dry ones; they did not have to swim one yard of the long, long trail.

The first remembered great rat plague thus appeared from the north, and after a 700 miles journey passed the outskirts of Broken Hill, New South Wales, in the early 1880s. Seldom indeed do these rodents reach the isolated Silver City, but on this occasion they just touched the frontiers of civilization. Travelling south-west the plague crossed the New South Wales border and vanished among the South Australian sandhills.

Coming seemingly from the skies, to vanish - where?

It is an Australian bush mystery. About every twenty years or so the plague suddenly comes out of the Far North to travel south fast for hundreds of miles, then gradually veer west towards the

Postcards showing the results of mice plagues in Australia May 1917.

Out in that lonely area station homesteads are far apart; travellers far and few between. Wherever one of these rat swarms crossed a track and a passing motorist came along his wheels simply crunched through or bounced over them. Then a few miles of clear track; then another swarm. And so on, until the traveller had crossed from one side of the plague to the other. Any horseman crossing such a plague patch had no uneasiness as regards speed. Once his horse got amongst the rats the difficulty was to hold him. The pests were not the ordinary city rat, but a brownish, smaller, more furry type. Their advance guard would reach a belt of green bushes lining the banks of a dry creek. They would simply mount the shrubs which would become bowed down as if under a swarm of gigantic bees. Soon the rats passed on and what had been bushes, now gleamed thin white sticks stripped of every vestige of bark. Skeleton bushes, skeleton roots; everything eatable was skeleton when the rats passed by.

As the vanguard of this plage sped on they drew towards the edge of the Simpson Desert until they were scurrying parallel with that desolation. No white man has ever crossed the centre of this small but truly terrible desert. No aboriginal even has crossed it. Into that desolation the explorer Leichhardt and his men are believed to have gone, never to be seen again. The vanguard reached the Cooper 700 miles south then veered in towards the Dead Heart and vanished. But the majority swarmed into the blood red sandhill s of the Simpson Desert.

What is the cause of these recurrent plagues? Where do the rats breed?

Why does it take them twenty years or more to breed up into the swarming stage? Why do they travel down the one line of semi-arid country? What causes them move at the psychological moment? What urge keeps them swiftly travelling? And what terrible safeguard of Nature forces them into the real Dead Heart where they vanish utterly.

# 12

# TRIP OUTBACK

*Series of Plagues. Homesteads engulfed by Sand.*

IN ADDITION to the drought, the settlers had to combat remarkable plagues of marching rats, which destroyed what was left of shrubs and herbage by millions of rabbits, and of cats which had gone wild. Added to those afflictions was a new terror shifting sand, which was so serious that it would become a national problem unless five or six good seasons came in succession to stop it.

I have been out four months. Because of the dry conditions it was a motor trip. I went along the south-west part of Queensland, along the Northern Territory border, the north of South Australia, and the north-west of New South Wales, through the dry country and along the Diamantina, the Georgina, and Cooper's Creek. One trip was down towards Lake Eyre until the sand-hill country got so bad that even the camels could not continue. The sand is smothering the country. It is rapidly getting worse. For 60 years, during which the sandhills country has been taken up, the land has had millions and millions of cattle and sheep over it. As it is a country of sparse rainfall and the herbage, though good, will only run one beast to every 25 square miles, year in and year out it deteriorates. Then, when countless millions of rabbits come along, not only the shrubs, but the roots also are eaten. After a few years of dry spells there are no roots left to grow the shrubs again. Then the winds come and the loosened sand is carried along. It begins to spread over hundreds of miles of country to such an extent that homesteads have been completely swamped, covered with sand, and abandoned. Water holes are filled up, and there is no water.

This was the condition of the country 200 miles north and east of Lake Eyre. The drift, he said, was now in south-western Queensland. It was already over the north of South Australia. It was beginning to spread over the north-west corner of New South Wales.

All the time, the drift is down towards the good country. Unless we have five or six good seasons in succession, so that the herbage can get started and get roots down and bind the sand, the trouble is going to be a national one.

## RATS LIKE A CARPET

The plague of countless millions of rats had gone over the sandhills spread out like a carpet, eating everything before them. They climbed shrubs where ever they found them, and the herbage waved under their weight. They stripped the bark from the shrubs and ate the roots, bringing the shrubs down. In many places they had completed the work the rabbits started. They stripped young mulga trees, ringbarking them. The rats had invaded homesteads and fowl-houses, eating the eggs. In some of the stations where saltbush was being kept for bad times to come, the rats went through the saltbush, what was left of the cotton bush, and even the cane grass, eating the roots so that they actually felled it and it died out.

These rats are a dirty brown colour, of the size of the warehouse rat. When they are there the ground seems to be moving. If you happen to be in a ear they won't get out of the way, and the wheels pass over a crunching mass of rat. They were very bad on the Diamantina and the Georgina. From the car, as far as we could see each side, were rats. None knows where they come from or where they disappear to. They have come three times in 18 months.

## CATS IN LEGIONS

Following the rats came thousands and thousands of cats. They are domestic cats that have gone bush and multiplied for generations. The majority are a reddish brown colour, At the homesteads where fowl runs were netted against dingoes they had also to be netted overhead against the cats. At one station on the Diamantina they shot 130 in one night, and that's a small number. They seem to stay thickly about the places where there is water, and catch birds. They are thinning out the bird life on the three great rivers, the Diamantina, the Georgina, and Cooper's Creek. So now the rats and cats have given the bushman something new to think about.

One notable point about the results of the hard times experienced outback, was that the modern drover was again using camels in carrying rations for horses as well as people. Drovers used camels at places where the stations were hard hit in getting stock from one water to another, so that droving had taken on a changed aspect.

## INLAND MISSION AND EDUCATION

Just two things stood out brightly in this last heart-breaking trip of mine. One was the work of the Australian Inland Mission, and the other the education by correspondence carried out by the Education Departments of each State. The A.I.M. sisters had their little hospitals crowded with fever cases, one sister to a hospital doing her best with the patients. Another rode hundreds of miles over gibber plains and parched sand to the farthest musterers' camps, and there injected all hands - white, coloured, and yellow - with the anti-typhoid vaccine. The sisters - city girls all of them - made these trips by station car where possible, by horse otherwise, in the localities where the horses were all dead, by camel.

Top: A stack caught at Crystal Brook, South Australia, 1917.
Below: Farmers take 200,000 mice at Pullut in Victoria, 1917.

And the people can't speak too highly of the education by correspondence. The mothers and fathers say: 'Droughts must come and go, but even through droughts we can now educate the children, and in the case of urgent sickness we have the little pedal transmitter that calls the 'Flying Doctor.' At every homestead I called at the children proudly showed me their lessons. Those women are very game. The accumulated dry seasons have meant dust-storms, stock dying, and not a blade of grass, and yet when you call in on them you'll be greeted with a smile and a 'Come in and have a cup of tea.' Yes; they're game. I hope these rains have reached them.

# 13

# Billy Turnbull

## *The Crusoe of Hicks Island*

*Mr W. Turnbull lessee of Hicks Island near Thursday Island declares that a Japanese tarn pun used his Island as a depot for crude oil supplies and that the Japanese stole some of his property. Residents of the Island he says will have to use firearms If they are not protected.*

So Billy Turnbull comes into the news! Throughout the Coral Sea he's known as the Crusoe of Hicks Island. A tall thin Australian is Billy with a drawl and a slow smile He walks his tiny beach in whites and a clean white helmet

Last time I was at Hicks' Island it was with Jardine, son of Jardine of Somerset. In a little cutter we were cruising the Great Barrier Reef. Billy was in a daze, for he had found a sapphire mine! He saw visions of London and Paris, caught a glimpse of fair maids of many lands. The sapphires were there all right but very few and very small. A geological puzzle, for a time the occurrence intrigued the officials of the far away Queensland Mines Department. One of the geologists had an interesting trip to inspect Billy's find. The sapphires were in blue clay among caverns of dead coral pushed up by the sea. A queer place. We would go crawling through these tiny tunnels and hear the moan of a sea coming from goodness knows where. It was a clammy feeling down there. We wondered what queer fishes must have chased one another through those subterranean galleries when that coral was being built down at the bottom of the sea.

Billy soon went back to his cocoanuts, the experimental sheep, and garden. He could not knock out a crust with these alone, so he had a little cutter and at seasonal times used to collect trochus from the reefs, with an occasional lucky find of pearlshell here and there. But Billy's cutter was wrecked. Billy's idea was to form an Australian cocoanut plantation, and while the trees were growing to grow produce for the distant pearling fleets of Thursday Island.

It is a lonely group, the Home Group, a cluster of little islets about twelve miles from the mainland of Cape York Peninsula. No whites on the mainland, Billy's only company a few nomad aborigines who would occasionally canoe across, and a South Sea Islander across on Haggerston Island, a few miles away. The nearest settlement is Thursday Island about 100 miles north. In the sou'-east season there is brilliant sunlight and sparkling seas, but with the nor'-west come the black squalls, the driving scuds of rain and occasionally the howling cyclone. Billy's little castle on the sea is a tiny house built on stilts. It is painted white and peeps out from among the dark-green mangroves on the tiniest of beaches.

## DANGEROUS PROWLERS

The high tides creep up under the house, and with them comes an occasional big crocodile. These prowlers raided Billy's pigsty, then one night they came in force, and the squeals of those suckers and sows and boar could hardly have been equalled by the howls in an imaginary Hades. To the splintering of breaking timber, the saurians smashed the sty, and all Billy's piglets went screaming back to the beach in the jaws of crocodiles.

Billy used to sit on his back step and blaze at the crawling shadows of the brutes when they invaded his fowl-house. The fowls made nearly as much noise as the pigs. One night Billy rolled straight back into his doorway as a noisome bulk loomed up from the steps at his feet. He

*Sydney Morning Herald*
*8-4-36*

## JAPANESE BOATS.

## Using Northern Island.

### LESSEE'S THREAT.

### "MAY HAVE TO USE FIREARMS."

BRISBANE, Friday.

Mr. W. Turnbull, lessee of Hicks Island, near Thursday Island, declares that a Japanese sampan used his island as a depot for crude oil supplies, and that the Japanese stole some of his property.

He has requested Mr. D. Riordan, M.P., to ask the Minister for Customs to obtain protection for a man named Charles Peters, who is employed by him on Haggerston Island, three miles from Hicks Island. Residents of the island, he says, will have to use firearms if they are not protected.

When he arrived at Thursday Island to-day, Mr. Turnbull said that on March 30 ten 40-gallon drums of crude oil, which had been left on Haggerston Island during the previous week by a sampan, were taken aboard another sampan, and that 100 empty kerosene tins were also removed.

He complained that the sampan crews, when they came ashore, were taking his goats and fruit from his orchard. He had seen local natives with quantities of Japanese tobacco.

A cutting from the Sydney Morning Herald, from the Idriess Archive.

barricaded the door and smashed a hole through the floor to poke his rifle through. But the steps collapsed under the beast as its claws scratched down the door.

Sir Hubert Wilkins was a guest of Billy's when Wilkins used his island as a base for his trip across the Peninsula. He got a beautiful collection of birds and butterflies from the island for some British museum. I hated the idea of those beautiful things destined for a museum, their song stilled for ever, their lovely wings no longer to flash under the kindly sun of the coral sea.

The island groups there are reef enclosed, their shores circled by mangroves, timbered with hardy timber and vine cluttered patches of scrub. Little hills, mostly grey. Bligh, in his great boat trip, sailed past there after he had got his first sight of the Australian coast at Restoration Rock. Hicks Island is the aboriginal "Spirit Island," a sacred island where the spirits come and dance. In places among its hillocks are bare rock patches a quarter-acre or so in extent, gleaming brown under the sun. These bare surfaces are marked out in queer designs with stones enclosing the different symbolic areas where different spirit groups come to commemorate dances they danced when in human form on earth. Hundreds of them dance there some nights on the anniversary of big festival seasons, according to the last of the natives. But the aborigines have died out on the island, as they almost have from the mainland opposite.

And so Billy Turnbull comes into the news, still the Crusoe of Hicks Island. He has been having trouble with the Japanese sampans. He and I together, in other years, have watched strange craft sail by his lonely island. Watched sail glide past on moonlit, nights that looked like a black shadow with moonlight glinting on a handkerchief. But I feel it a shame somehow; Billy is a nice, quiet chap, well educated, a kindly man. He would make a wonderful husband, and yet there he is all alone, for long periods, even without a man Friday.

ETT IMPRINT has the following ION IDRIESS books in print in 2024:

Prospecting for Gold (1931)
Lasseter's Last Ride (1931)
Flynn of the Inland (1932)
The Desert Column (1932)
Men of the Jungle (1932)
Drums of Mer (1933)
Gold-Dust and Ashes (1933)
The Yellow Joss (1934)
Man Tracks (1935)
Over the Range (1937)
Forty Fathoms Deep (1937)
Madman's Island (1938)
Headhunters of the Coral Sea (1940)
Lightning Ridge (1940)
Nemarluk (1941)
Shoot to Kill (1942)
Sniping (1942)
Guerrilla Tactics (1942)
Trapping the Jap (1942)
Lurking Death (1942)
The Scout (1943)
Horrie the Wog Dog (1945)
The Opium Smugglers (1948)
The Wild White Man of Badu (1950)
Outlaws of the Leopolds (1952) The
Red Chief (1953)
The Vanished People (1955)
The Silver City (1956)
Coral Sea Calling (1957)
Back O' Cairns (1958)
The Wild North (1960)
Tracks of Destiny (1961)
Gouger of the Bulletin (2013)
Ion Idriess: The Last Interview (2020)
Ion Idriess Letters (2023)